Getting the Most Out of Mozart

Unlocking the Masters Series, No. 3

Getting the Most
Out of Mozart
The Instrumental Works

David Hurwitz

AMADEUS
PRESS

Pompton Plains, NJ • Cambridge, UK

Published in 2005 by

Amadeus Press, LLC
512 Newark Pompton Turnpike
Pompton Plains, New Jersey 07444, USA

Amadeus Press
2 Station Road
Swavesey, Cambridge CB4 5QJ, UK

For sales, please contact

NORTH AMERICA

AMADEUS PRESS, LLC
c/o Hal Leonard Corp.
7777 West Bluemound Road
Milwaukee, Wisconsin 53213, USA
Tel. 800-637-2852
Fax 414-774-3259

UNITED KINGDOM AND EUROPE

AMADEUS PRESS
2 Station Road
Swavesey, Cambridge CB4 5QJ, UK
Tel. 01954-232959
Fax 01954-206040

E-mail: orders@amadeuspress.com
Website: www.amadeuspress.com

Printed in Canada

Library of Congress Cataloging-in-Publication Data

Hurwitz, David, 1961–
Getting the most out of Mozart : the instrumental works / by David Hurwitz.— 1st paperback ed.
      p. cm. — (Unlocking the masters series ; no. 3)
    Includes index.
    ISBN 1-57467-096-4
     1. Mozart, Wolfgang Amadeus, 1756-1791. Instrumental music. 2. Instrumental music—Analysis, appreciation. I. Title. II. Series.

  MT92.M7H87 2005
  784'.092—dc22

2004018847

To Caroline, Ben, and Jack

Contents

Part 3: Orchestral Music

Part 4: Concertos

Preface
Selecting the Best of Mozart

The standard catalogue of Mozart's works, assembled by musicologist Ludwig Köchel, originally contained 626 items, representing an amazing achievement in sheer volume for a composer who died at age thirty-five. Each work accordingly is tagged with a "K" number, reflecting what Köchel believed to be the original order of composition, and this makes identification scientifically accurate on the whole. I say "on the whole" because subsequent revisions and changes to Köchel's chronology in light of later scholarship and new discoveries have led to some works being renumbered or receiving multiple "K" numbers. This silly habit is pointlessly confusing (better simply to make a new chronological catalogue and be done with it), as is the fact that although works such as the symphonies are consecutively numbered (1–41), Mozart wrote closer to sixty symphonies, with all of those after No. 41 (the "Jupiter") actually coming earlier and thus having lower "K" numbers.

In the following discussion, I will give more than enough information to identify each work in question. If you don't see a "K" number, it's because the piece is one of a kind and no confusion can arise. When I use "K" numbers it's for convenience, and to keep things as simple as possible, I will often omit mention of key (C major, G minor, and so forth) unless I regard this as useful information as well. So there's no need to worry if some works have nicknames, others are famous single pieces in the genre in question (like the Clarinet Quintet), still others have "K" numbers and/or key designations, and the symphonies and piano concertos have unique numbering systems, from 1 to 41 and from 1 to 27 respectively. In each case, what you see is all that you'll need to know in order to find your way through Mozart's highly varied musical landscape.

How does one choose from the enormous quantity of excellent, truly representative music available? I have adopted several criteria that I think result in a fair, representative, and generous selection of pieces that not only covers the range of Mozart's achievement but leaves ample scope for individual listeners to follow their own inclinations based on what they find within these pages:

1. I have included as many works as possible that are important landmarks in Mozart's musical development, in the history of music in general, or in the history of their respective genres.

2. The ease of obtaining recordings matters; after all, if you can't listen to the music, there's not much point in my talking about it. With titles going in and out of print almost daily and obscure items the most likely to vanish suddenly, I necessarily focus on works with decent catalogue longevity and a wide range of available interpretations ready to hand.

3. I have tried to take into account the musical consensus (as I understand it) that has coalesced around Mozart's best work. After all, more than 200 years of scholarly activity, ongoing public performance, and cultural debate can't be all wrong.

4. I have decided not to cover those genres in which the most noteworthy features of the works in question are evidenced just as well by looking at other, more highly acclaimed examples of his output.

This means for example that I will not be discussing Mozart's solo piano works, even though some (such as the "Turkish" Rondo in the Sonata K. 331 and the Sonata in C, K. 545) are very popular, while others (the Fantasia in C Minor, K. 475, and the sonatas K. 457, 570, 576, and 533/494) are generally acknowledged as "great" Mozart. So too are the magnificent sonatas for two pianos or piano duo, K. 448, 497, and 521 respectively, which really are landmarks in this sadly neglected medium. Still, Mozart's genius as a composer for the piano is best expressed by general consent in his piano concertos, which I will discuss very extensively (more than a dozen). Similarly, the violin sonatas and piano trios, fine as some of them are, can be just as easily understood and enjoyed by looking at other great chamber works with piano (such as the two piano quartets).

In the field of orchestral music, Mozart's concertos for clarinet and flute cover the "concerto for orchestra and wind instrument" category very well, even though horn players and bassoonists may disagree. Similarly, Mozart wrote five violin concertos, but discussion of two (plus the Sinfonia Concertante for Violin and Viola) will be sufficient. Of the numerous serenades and divertimentos, I have selected some of the best and most popular (yes, *Eine Kleine Nachtmusik* is here!), and when it comes to symphonies, despite the recent fetish (on discs at least) for complete editions, Nos. 25, 29, 31, and 35–41 will do nicely. On the other hand, some of Mozart's finest orchestral pieces are his opera overtures, so it makes sense to include a number of them as well, and I think you'll be very happy that I did.

If you're curious about how old Mozart was when he composed the pieces in this book (and who isn't?), keep in mind that he was born in 1756. Our survey of the chamber and orchestral music begins, chronologically speaking, with

Symphony No. 25, composed in 1773 when he was just seven-teen, and continues right up to his death in 1791—a total of just eighteen years.

Getting the Most
Out of Mozart

Part 1

Mozart's Musical Identity and Personal Style

Introduction
Two Mozarts

If you are attracted to a piece by Mozart and decide to start listening to more of his music, you may well find yourself bewildered by the sheer volume of recordings available and the range of material that seems to be in the active repertoire of today's classical music performers. This wasn't always the case. Fifty years ago, the only Mozart that you needed to care about consisted of about half a dozen symphonies, a dozen or so concertos for various instruments (mostly piano), perhaps five operas, two or three sacred works, and a small handful of chamber pieces in the quartet and quintet genres—and even that (assuming you wanted to hear it all) would have been considered taking things to the outer limits of enthusiasm.

Today, on the other hand, with at least two complete recorded editions and innumerable boxed sets containing all the sacred works, symphonies, concertos, chamber works, and even operas, listeners are confronted with more than 600 pieces, any one of which can be pretty easily found magnificently played and beautifully presented by any number of concert organizations and record labels. The proliferation of chamber orchestras, soloists, and chamber ensembles playing "period instruments" and the ease of making compact discs have led to a deluge of minor Mozart, all marketed under the assumption that it must all be equally great.

There are in fact two Mozarts, one an extremely precocious and competent general musician and craftsman, while the other remains one of the most astounding musical geniuses that ever lived. Mozart was gifted with prodigious talent and, even more importantly (as Haydn pointed out to the composer's father), "taste, and the most thorough knowledge of composition." He had the good fortune to be the recipient of an outstanding musical education from his father and to be working within accepted stylistic parameters that created music of astonishingly high quality simply by following the rules and copying the best examples extant of any particular form or genre. This is how Mozart the craftsman got by when necessary—and it was often very necessary. A good deal of what he wrote is very good classical-period music, but it's not great Mozart.

On the other hand, there are dozens of works (some would even say hundreds) that really are great Mozart. Somewhere between the traditional "cream of the crop" approach and the current mania for "it's all wonderful" complete editions lies a body of work unique in style, expressive range, emotional depth, formal perfection, and sheer surface beauty. Listen, for example, just to the first minute of Symphony No. 40 on your accompanying CD (track 2). This music, with its special combination of grace and nervous intensity, doesn't sound like anyone else's. No one but Mozart could have written it; his musical fingerprints stand out like the telltale evidence at a crime scene. The only special equipment you need to uncover this evidence is a sympathetic pair of ears allied to sufficient time for relaxed recreational listening.

So without attempting to address the thorny philosophical question of what constitutes "greatness," this book will attempt to answer a different and more practical question: which works give us the essence of "Mozartness?" In order to do this, we have to try to pin down what qualities Mozart brings to our musical table that make him so special in the first place, and this is both easier and harder than you might think. It's easy because there's a remarkable consensus with respect to his music about which almost everyone agrees: what distinguishes Mozart's works above all else (expressively speaking) is their humanity. His music is "about" people; even his instrumental music treats melodies like characters in a play or opera, and in all his best pieces, these characters come alive. They laugh, cry, live, die, and evolve through their experiences over the course of a given movement or work.

You will not hear in Mozart's instrumental music any important references to the world of nature, for example. There are no storms, bird calls, or animal sounds, such as fascinated his contemporaries Haydn and Beethoven. Nor will you find a shred of religious feeling in Mozart, if one means by this a self-conscious attempt to contrast the puny insignificance of mankind with musical evocations of divine glory or spiritual transcendence. In fact, despite the popularity of his unfinished Requiem (a job he took on for the money), Mozart spent a good bit of his career actively trying not to write religious music of any kind. What you will hear in his music, then, is a veritable catalogue of human emotions, and when it does indulge in descriptive imagery, what Mozart most often describes is human activity: marching, dancing, the hunt, a quarrel, or falling in love.

In this respect, Mozart truly was unique. Think of all the music that is valued because of its descriptive qualities: Vivaldi's *The Four Seasons*, Tchaikovsky's *1812 Overture*, Beethoven's *Pastoral Symphony*, or Haydn's "Lark" String Quartet. The effort to exploit music's ability to evoke nature, or to depict epic events such as heroic battles and tragic defeats, has been a major preoccupation of composers for centuries. None of this has any significant place in Mozart's world. His heroes are characters like the barber Figaro, and his music cuts everyone down to the same size, even the aristocrats, because in the end (he seems to be telling us), everyone is created equal.

Despite this general agreement on Mozart's expressive focus, describing exactly how his instrumental music achieves it can be difficult. In an opera (or vocal music in general), where the words tell listeners what the music means and the music in turn fleshes out the characters of the protagonists, this isn't such a problem. Instrumental music, on the other hand, usually sends commentators running for the shelter of technical jargon or biographical explanations, for the simple reason that describing what any piece of abstract music "means" or even "sounds like" is inherently subjective and often elusive. It is sometimes much easier to look at the composer's life and martial evidence of what is known about that composer's thoughts and feelings when writing any given work, or to talk about a wonderful modulation from the key of G minor to E-flat major, because these are facts and not opinions or interpretations.

If, however, we have the courage of our convictions and truly believe that Mozart was a genius and that his music is great because it communicates across the centuries with a certain degree of universality, the reason for this phenomenon ought to be describable in terms of what normal listeners hear—as a series of easily audible musical characteristics. There's a very foolish notion prevailing in the classical music world that great works must necessarily be difficult, complicated, or fragile, and that the slightest misstep on the part of the performer or a moment's inattention on the part of the listener means that its message invariably gets lost. It's an all or nothing proposition. The reality, though, is precisely the opposite. Classical music in general, and Mozart's in particular, is as hardy as a weed. It has survived this long, and it communicates with remarkable success no matter what anyone does to it. Were this not true, it would not have become a "classic" in the first place.

So first of all, trust the strength of Mozart's music. Second, I agree to use only as much technical terminology as is necessary to describe how to get the most out of it. Third, I want to avoid irrelevant speculation about what Mozart may have thought or said at any given time and instead focus your attention entirely on how the music actually sounds. Mozart's music achieves its special human qualities because of his special gift at characterization, of writing music that sings like a human voice and flows like conversation, whether witty, contentious, bantering, or pleading. This vocal quality relies for its success on Mozart's command of orchestration and instrumental color, on his ability to energize his musical textures both vertically (that is, using harmony and counterpoint) and horizontally (that is, rhythmically), to articulate his ideas in satisfying formal structures, and above all on his gift for writing gorgeous, expressively varied melodies.

All these qualities manifest themselves whenever you listen to one of Mozart's works, and they aren't difficult either to describe or to hear. There's a huge difference between a composer whose work is subtle and smart, which Mozart's certainly is, and one whose work is impenetrable or obscure, which Mozart's definitely is not. In fact, the greatest barrier to a deeper enjoyment of his music is its sheer surface beauty and often childlike simplicity of utterance: it's so easy on the ear that sometimes it can sound uniformly pleasant (and therefore tensionless and dull). This problem often leads both listeners and commentators to overcompensate in the other direction, ascribing huge importance to tiny differences between works or movements, resulting in the "it's all equally wonderful" mentality so prevalent today. Moreover, the wide popularity of certain less than first-rank works, such as the Concerto for Flute and Harp (because it's both pretty and the only important harp solo by any major classical-period composer) and the incomplete, posthumously published Requiem (much of which isn't by Mozart at all) further muddies the waters.

Getting the most out of Mozart really doesn't require so much effort or demand that you turn off your critical faculties and feel guilty for preferring some works over others. I will help you avoid these pitfalls through the simple expedient of giving you the tools you need to listen sympathetically, to make informed choices, and to select your own favorites from among the hundreds of works that Mozart left to posterity, always keeping in mind that Mozart was not some mythical being but a person—however talented—with enough in common with the rest of us that there is no conflict between the universal feelings and emotions that his music evokes and the very personal musical style he developed in order to evoke them. So without further delay, let's get to know that style.

Musical Form
in the Classical Period

Whenever the subject of musical form comes up, two reactions are common in most listeners: fear and boredom. The fear comes from the mistaken assumption that musical forms are complicated constructs created by theoreticians and used by composers the way great chefs use detailed recipes, following some obscure predetermined plan that guarantees success every time for a trained staff in the restaurant but that normal food lovers could never hope to duplicate in their kitchens at home. The boredom stems from the fact that questions of form often seem irrelevant to the main reason that most people listen to music in the first place: to experience the spontaneous expression of feelings and emotions. Neither reaction is justified, for two basic reasons.

First, musical forms arise organically as a means of organizing and focusing the feelings and emotions that music expresses. This is especially true of Mozart, because one aspect of his greatness lies in the fact that not only did he use existing musical forms, he invented (or perfected) new ones. So his approach to form, as often as not, is as spontaneous as any other aspect of his art. And despite his great love of balance and symmetry in the way he organizes each work, Mozart's best pieces never sound stiff, contrived, or formulaic. This isn't to say that his use of form isn't sophisticated or that his music isn't complex, but for Mozart, as for most great composers, formal success is inseparable from expressive success, and he never purchases the former at the expense of the latter.

Second, not only is musical form necessary and inevitable in composition, you understand as much of it as you need simply through listening. Every time you recognize a theme or motive that you have heard before, you have noticed some aspect of musical form at work. When you consciously or unconsciously register the contrast between slow music and fast, loud passages and soft ones, strings and brass, or a solo instrument and the full orchestra, you participate actively in the unfolding of a musical form—even if the specific type or kind of form is new to you. In fact, if you like any piece of music at all, part of your enjoyment stems from your innate appreciation of its form (particularly that aspect of form that lets you feel that the work is exactly the right length and therefore not too long, too short, or just plain boring).

That said, it stands to reason that over time certain formal types occur frequently enough to have earned names that describe them, and it makes sense to know them because it makes talking about the music much easier and puts listeners everywhere on the same footing. After all, even if I could be scientifically precise and say "the tune at 2:12 into the finale" of a given work, that would only be true of a single performance, and there are dozens, if not hundreds, of versions available on disc of Mozart's most popular pieces, no two of which are exactly alike as regards tempos and timings.

So if I say "the second subject of the exposition," it is true that you may not be able to find the exact spot on your own recording right away, but you will know that I'm talking about a moment occurring within the first few minutes of a movement in sonata form, a bit after the appearance of its opening theme. This method also has the advantage of encouraging you to listen to movements and works whole and to hear passages in context. In a narrative musical style such as Mozart's, which thrives on the contrast produced by a linear succession of musical events over time, this is critically important, as well as very enjoyable. And because we can listen together to the extensive musical examples on the compact disc included with this book, allowing me to give exact timings down to the second, you can be sure that you will know what all of the formal terms mean and how Mozart's musical structures work—useful knowledge that you can apply not just to Mozart's music but to that of other composers as well.

Still, it's important never to mistake the point of learning these names (so that one can describe the music efficiently in words) with the need to know them in order to understand the music (a process that happens automatically in the course of listening). Even those works that make a point of highlighting some especially interesting or moving (yes, form can be expressive) aspect of their musical construction—and there are quite a few in Mozart—don't require extensive knowledge of specific formal types and processes any more than enjoying the graceful outlines of the Eiffel Tower requires an insider's knowledge of welding and structural engineering.

The following discussion, then, will allow us to talk about Mozart's music according to a consistent and generally accepted terminology that you will often encounter well beyond the confines of this book. As soon as you have the main musical forms that Mozart used and enriched under your belt, you will be able to see clearly that form as used by Mozart is not an expressive straightjacket but rather the tool that sets the artist free, allowing each new work to tell its own story and reveal its uniqueness to the listener in the most immediate and effective way.

The list of formal types below moves from the most simple to the most complex.

ABA

This means just what it looks like: an initial section, then a middle section, then a return to the opening section in identical or slightly modified form. Extremely common and effective, this basic musical form is popular in movements of dancelike character and movements in slow tempos, where it is often called *song form*. The reason it works so well in slow movements is that musically speaking "slow" means "long," and the simple alternation of one slow melody with another, followed by the return of the initial melody, can create a perfectly satisfying whole several minutes in length with no need for further elaboration. You can hear this for yourself in the exquisite and very popular slow movement of Piano Concerto No. 21 on CD track 3. In all such cases, highlighting the beauty of the tunes is the entire object of the form. Even more important, though, is this basic form's use in dance music, and in particular:

The Minuet

The dance most commonly found in Mozart's instrumental music is the minuet, a precursor of the waltz, and when it appears in a symphony or chamber work, it is almost invariably one of the middle movements (second or third in a typical four-movement scheme) or very occasionally a light finale. The A section usually consists of a tune in two halves, both of which get repeated, and the same is true of B, which is called for some odd historical reason a trio. The word *trio* in this context has nothing to do with the number three. It just means "middle section of a dance movement." The A section, when it returns, often omits the repeats, but this is largely a matter of choice on the part of the performer. You can find one of Mozart's most buoyant minuets on track 9 of the accompanying CD. This one comes from Symphony No. 39, and its trio (at 2:03) is a delicious bit of carnival music featuring the two clarinets as soloists.

The purpose of the minuet, as you can very well imagine, is to provide contrast, by reason of its rhythmic regularity as well as its melodic and harmonic simplicity when compared to the other movements, most of which will be longer and more highly developed. Sometimes a composer will write more than one trio and repeat the minuet between them, as Mozart does for example in his Clarinet Quintet. When this happens, the form becomes ABACA, and overlaps with another very popular type of movement:

The Rondo

Rondos are very popular as the finales of symphonies, concertos, and chamber works of all sorts, for reasons I'll touch on a bit later. In a rondo, the A section, or main theme that always comes back, is called a *ritornello,* while the subsidiary sections are called *episodes.* Like the minuet, the ritornello theme often has two halves, both of which usually get repeated (at least on initial presentation). There can be any number of episodes separated by the ritornello, depending on how long the composer wants the movement to be, and musically speaking, anything can happen in an episode. For example the "Turkish" interlude in the finale of Mozart's Fifth Violin Concerto, so vivid that it actually gave the entire work its nickname ("Turkish" Concerto), is an episode in a rondo. One of Mozart's zaniest creations is also a rondo, the finale of the "Gran Partita" for wind instruments, on track 10 of your accompanying CD.

Variations

All musical form depends on repetition and variation to some extent, but some movements (or entire works) adopt the process of variation as the point of their existence. In these cases the movement will open with the variation theme, again usually presented in two halves, both repeated. Here the repetition has an important additional formal point aside from helping you to remember the tune, because each of the following variations will also typically fall into two halves, both repeated, only some of these repeats will also be varied even further. When this happens, the variation is called a *double variation*. Slow movements and finales may be prime candidates for variation form. Some of Mozart's most famous sets of variations include the finale of his Clarinet Quintet, the finales of the Seventeenth and Twenty-fourth Piano Concertos, and the delightful variations K. 265/300e for solo piano on the French folk song "Ah, Vous Dirai-Je Maman" (better known today as "Twinkle, Twinkle Little Star").

On the whole, though, while you will find the variation principal widely used by Mozart, he did not write very many full-fledged variation sets in his larger works, for the simple reason that the sectional nature of the form, with each variation a more or less independent unit, tends to create a "stop and go" impression that checks the music's forward progress. In three of the works just mentioned, the presence of a genuine solo (clarinet or piano) with a strongly contrasting instrumental timbre to the larger group (string quartet or orchestra) offers sufficient variety to justify the form that Mozart uses—as does his creativity as a variation writer. In general, though, Mozart prefers less rigid forms that permit him to explore bigger and more highly differentiated musical paragraphs.

The main theme, or *subject,* of most variations often will be very simple and catchy—perhaps a folk song or nursery rhyme, or even a popular tune by another composer—so that you can recognize it whenever it returns and follow those variations that stick closely to the shape of the melody. It is important to recognize, however, that quite often what a composer may be developing in writing a variation is not the melody at all but its rhythm, phrase structure, or harmonic foundation (or any combination of these), and when this happens, you won't be able to hear any clear resemblance to the original tune. Such variations exist exactly for this purpose: to provide a change of pace, and whenever Mozart (or any good variation writer) wants you to recognize the subject, rest assured that you will. Never worry about it when you don't. I will look at this form more fully in the next chapter, but if you want to hear an especially characterful example of a variation movement, try track 4 on your accompanying CD, which is the finale of Piano Concerto No. 17 in G Major.

Contrapuntal Forms

Counterpoint is the art of combining independent musical lines (called *voices*), and music written according to the rules of counterpoint is termed *polyphonic* (many-voiced). Polyphonic instrumental music was one of the great achievements of the baroque period, and its greatest practitioners were Bach and Handel. The most important contrapuntal form is the fugue, and you will seldom encounter one in Mozart's instrumental music. A fugue consists of a theme (the subject) played successively in turn by however many voices the composer chooses to use (usually three to five). Each presentation or *exposition* of the subject is separated by episodes of varying character, much as in a rondo, although the subject will usually be altered when it comes back in any number of ways: it can be played upside down (or *inverted*), backwards, in longer or shorter notes, or any combination of these tactics.

The general musical impression that fugues produce is rhe-torical: of a discussion or argument among several simultaneous participants. On the other hand, the classical style as perfected by Mozart was not rhetorical in nature: it was dramatic. In other words, instead of exploring the vertical complexity of contra-puntal instrumental textures, Mozart's method creates a linear or horizontal progression of highly contrasted musical events, and his textures are *homophonic*—which means melodies with subordinate accompaniments.

In this context, counterpoint becomes an important element of textural contrast, one which Mozart seized with relish. So rather than turning his back on the baroque tradition, it's prob-ably fairer to say that he absorbed it and found new uses for it within the context of the newly emerging classical style. Chamber music, especially the string quartets and quintets, offered Mozart particularly fruitful opportunities to explore this new synthesis, while the finale of the "Jupiter" Symphony remains one of the very greatest examples of counterpoint placed in the service of a dramatic orchestral movement.

The Sonata Concept

The word *sonata* (to sound together) has meant different things at different times in musical history. As developed by Haydn, Mozart, and Beethoven, it can be considered a medium, a form, and a style—the classical style in fact. Taken as a whole, the "Sonata Concept" constitutes the most flexible and adaptable musical system ever invented: one still very much with us today. Despite many predictions of its decline and obsolescence, it has never been supplanted, although it has been ineptly used or mis-understood subsequent to its invention by less-than-brilliant later composers (no period in history ever has any shortage of those).

So it pays to spend some time understanding what it is and how it works as it applies to Mozart's music.

Sonata: The Medium

A sonata in the classical period is simply any multi-movement instrumental work, usually (but not always) having at least one of those movements in *sonata form* (see below). Works for one or two instruments are usually simply called sonatas of some type (sonata for solo piano = "piano sonata," sonata for violin and piano = "violin sonata," and so forth). More than two instruments and one encounters trios, quartets, quintets, sextets, and so forth, but all of these are also sonatas. A *concerto* is a sonata for solo instrument with orchestra, and a sonata for orchestra alone is called a *symphony* (or in Mozart's day, often an *overture*). Mozart wrote important sonatas in every single one of these various media and genres. As long as you understand that the term basically applies to all instrumental music, save some stand-alone single movements and a few exceptions such as groups of dances (*suites*), independent sets of variations, or works in purely contrapuntal forms (such as fugues), I don't need to explore this particular aspect of the term any further.

Sonata: The Form

All a composer needs to write a movement in sonata form is two tunes, two keys, and a good imagination. Okay, I'm oversimplifying, but while commentators and scholars pore over the endless permutations and subtleties of serious music's most popular and widely used form, it pays to point out one obvious fact: the reason it is so popular is because it's fundamentally so practical and natural-sounding.

A movement in sonata form has two halves containing a total of three sections. The first half of the movement contains the exposition section, in which the composer presents two subjects, the first in the home key (or *tonic*) and the second usually in the key most closely related to the tonic (a fifth above, or the *dominant*). There are no rules over what can go into either first or second subjects: they may consist of a single melody or many melodies, long tunes or tiny motives, or even the same tunes and motives different only in arrangement or instrumentation, and all of this in any proportion. The reason the second subject usually occurs in the dominant (or some key other than "home") is simple: a journey of a thousand miles begins with the first step, and so this step needs to be long enough to give a clear impression of movement "away," but not so long as to sound capricious, incoherent, or unrelated to what has come before.

This inherent flexibility means that no two expositions are exactly the same as regards both content and the way that they can be presented and organized. In fact there is a wide range of scholarly opinion about such issues as where exactly the "second subject" begins in relationship to its surroundings. In other words, the terminology describing musical forms and sections is vague and only serves to describe very general principles. However, you can rest assured that every exposition in a sonata movement effectively sets the scene for what follows. That is its job. On your sample CD (track 1), the exposition section of the "Jupiter" Symphony's first movement lasts from the beginning until 3:02.

The second half of the movement contains two sections. The first of these is the *development* (in the "Jupiter" Symphony, this runs from 6:04 until 7:44), in which the composer combines material in different ways, either from the first or second subjects or from the often voluminous transitional material between them, moving through different keys in the process. Again, there are no rules about what, if anything, a composer has to use in his development. More than a few (including some famous ones by Mozart) ignore the themes of the exposition almost completely, making their ultimate return all the more refreshing as a result. This return is called the *recapitulation section* (beginning at 7:45 and lasting until the end of the movement), and its job is to reestablish the tonic by playing both subjects in the home key. Doing this usually involves a good bit of recomposition, because the music that previously led to the dominant key now has to be reworked to remain in the tonic. Sometimes this leads to exten-sive passages of further development, and it may require a coda to provide a satisfying climax and ending.

And this is basically all you need to know about sonata form. Mozart uses it in his mature work more than just about any other composer, not only in first movements, but in slow movements and finales too. He literally couldn't get enough of it, and because his use of sonata structure is so clear and so frequent, his per-sonal style has in fact become the textbook exemplar of a form that he never even knew by its common name (the term *sonata form* was created by a German theorist decades after Mozart's death). Mozart's use of sonata form is in any case, anything but predictable. Still, there are some stylistic habits characteristic of the fully fledged Mozartean sonata that may be useful to know, as long as one considers them tendencies or inclinations and not invariable rules. These are:

1. Mozart seldom writes introductions to sonata movements as many other composers do. He almost always starts immedi-ately with his first subject.
2. Mozart tends to write very full (that is, long and equally important) first and second subjects, and he often makes the

contrast between them as great as possible, even separating them from each other by a general pause—almost the musical equivalent of a train making a stop before moving on to the next station.

3. Mozart likes symmetrical endings; in other words, he doesn't often write long codas to wrap up his movements, preferring instead to end a movement in a manner similar to the end of the exposition (which often brings back a bit of the opening theme or motive in condensed form for good measure). The resultant abruptness paradoxically gives the music a severely logical sense of finality, of "there's nothing more to say, so there!"

4. Mozart enhances many a movement's formal symmetry by repeating *both* halves, something you will seldom hear in performance, since tradition dictates that exposition repeats be observed and so-called second-half repeats be ignored. The reason: repeating the almost invariably longer second half of a sonata movement can make it very long indeed and also undermine (to some ears, anyway) the finality of the ending. This is very much a subjective impression and one that involves personal taste. Once you are familiar with the music, you can decide for yourself what position (if any) you take on the "repeat issue." I find it a question that really needs to be looked at on a case-by-case basis, depending on the work itself as well as the performer's interpretation.

5. In movements that begin in minor (sad, uneasy, tense) keys, instead of following the usual custom of ending in the major (happy, comfortable) version of the same key, Mozart prefers to remain in the minor. This is a perfect example of how a severely logical approach to the rules of the form produces a result even more expressive, poignant, and dramatically powerful than many a more theoretically free approach. I'll explore this point further in the next chapter.

You can hear every one of these tendencies or predilections in the first movement of Mozart's G Minor Symphony, K. 550 (CD track 2). This piece has always served as an exemplar for Mozart's personal treatment of sonata form; it has also served equally as one of the most famous examples of Mozart's highly individual melodic style, gift for orchestration, and expressive depth and power. In short, the idea that composers can write in "great forms" without having equally great ideas in all other respects is nonsense. A movement such as this is all of a piece, and if you listen to the whole thing, you can't help but be struck by its remarkable sense of completeness and inevitability, of which form as such is merely one aspect of the totality.

The above remarks, then, lay out the basics of sonata form as a kind of musical architecture. However, in order to understand why Mozart's mastery of sonata form matters so much, one needs to dig a little deeper into its fundamental principles.

The Sonata Style

I mentioned previously that contrapuntal forms such as fugues were "rhetorical" or "argumentative," while sonata forms are "dramatic." Most explanations of sonata form end with this point of contrast. They will tell you the form is dramatic, but they won't tell you *why*. The answer is actually very straightforward, and you don't need a degree in music theory to understand it. Rondos, variations, minuets, and fugues all work formally by arranging any number of self-contained sections according to certain established patterns of repetition and alternation. It is the idea of "departure and return." They almost invariably end by bringing back their opening theme, because the repetition of a well-remembered tune after any number of partial statements or interruptions offers the opportunity for a natural and compelling climax and thus a satisfying conclusion. For example, even the variation finale of Piano Concerto No. 17, which has a huge coda based on an entirely new theme, brings back the opening tune at the very end (CD track 4 at 7:42).

A sonata movement also depends on this same idea of departure and return, except that rather than departing from and returning to a specific tune, what matters equally in sonata form is the return to the initially chosen tonality, or key. By selecting a particular key as home, the melodies (or subjects) in a sonata-form movement take on the guise of characters that are presented, evolve, and return changed by their experiences in the course of the movement. Not only is this dramatic, it is *inevitably* dramatic, if for no other reason than the fact that most sonata-form movements will not end with their opening themes if the composer sticks to the initial order of presentation, and so he needs to find another (or additional) method for achieving formal closure.

So by the standards of the forms discussed previously, sonata structure de-emphasizes the importance of the single, movement-defining initial melody in favor of a more democratic assortment of thematic material arranged over a sequence of keys, and this parade of ideas is inherently open-ended and incomplete unless something musically dramatic happens. This has two critical consequences for an artist who knows how to use the form well, both of which result in thrilling music:

Consequence I

In order to achieve the expected feeling of finality to sonata-movement endings, it is absolutely necessary to emphasize the fact of being home when the recapitulation arrives. The reworking of the second subject, then, to stay in the opening key of the movement isn't some capricious whim or arbitrarily rigid rule:

it's truly the only way that you will ever believe that the end of the movement is approaching and feel satisfied when it finally happens. So when the ideas of the second subject get recomposed after the volatile development section, the reassertion of tonal stability has a feeling of organic inevitability and purpose, because the only way to return home is for the music to actually *change*. It cannot merely repeat itself literally. Although you may not be conscious of it, you cannot help but feel the underlying logic and sense the forward progress of this process as it happens in real time.

Consequence 2

It is entirely possible, and indeed not at all uncommon, for a composer to wish to end a sonata movement with the opening theme or in some other fashion entirely. This involves two choices: changing the order of the recapitulation or adding a coda. Both only increase the drama, because the obligation to provide a satisfying tonal balance remains as strong as ever. For example, beginning the recapitulation with the second subject is going to require even more recomposition (that is, adjustments to the themes and transitions) than playing the two subjects in their original order. Adding a coda, if not to sound pointlessly redundant, means delaying the final assertion of tonal stability, and so it inevitably requires a certain amount of additional development and suspense, and this can be hugely exciting musically (probably the most famous example is the positively shattering coda of the first movement of Beethoven's Fifth Symphony).

So just as a story can have an infinite number of plotlines and still be called a novel or a play, so organizing the musical process of departure and return by tonal means can be achieved in innumerable ways and still be an example of sonata form. This provides limitless opportunities to absorb the widest range of musical materials and present them in ways that are not just unexpected and surprising but that also require musical change and development in order to achieve completion. Isn't this also what drama does? Characters (or in music, subjects) participate in a connected series of actions, the ultimate result of which you don't know until the story reaches a satisfying ending—the consequence of all that has come before. Mozart is one of music's greatest storytellers, and if the music is *abstract* (that is, has no words), then the story will be one of feelings and emotions, but no less intriguing or suspenseful for that.

Tips for Listening

From the listener's point of view, there are two very important additional considerations arising from the frequent use of sonata form in multi-movement orchestral and chamber works.

One, they get bigger, and in music this means longer. Mozart's mature orchestral and chamber works stand among the grandest of any era. Most large works in the classical period (including virtually all of Mozart's) put the sonata-form movement first, because it's the longest and most complex one. Where Mozart parts company with his lesser colleagues is in what happens next. Traditionally, the work relaxes after the opening "sonata." Each succeeding movement adopts one of the simpler forms that I have just described. No matter how fast and brilliant the finale, for example, a rondo will always sound "lighter" than a sonata movement because of the absence of development, the frequency of literal repetition of the main theme (or ritornello), and the episodic nature of the form. Even though Mozart customarily respects the idea of a progressive lightening of tone as a piece proceeds, he also has no qualms about writing a four-movement work in which two or three of the movements are in some version of sonata form (as you will see, there are several comparatively simple varieties), and the resultant increase in length can be very striking.

To put this into perspective, the average concerto of a baroque composer such as Vivaldi has three movements and will last between nine and twelve minutes. In a mature three-movement Mozart piano concerto, twenty-five to thirty minutes is closer to average (as indeed it remains in similar works written today), with as much as half of this time belonging to the opening movement in sonata form. In the late symphonies, quartets, and quintets, which generally have four movements—several in sonata form—a playing time of thirty to thirty-five minutes isn't unusual (depending on the treatment of repeats). Don't worry though: in all the music I will be discussing, Mozart uses the extra time to excellent effect.

Two, the mere act of describing the three main sections of a movement in sonata form may lead you to worry about "where" you are in it. Was that tune you just heard part of the first or second subject? Is this the development? When does the recapitulation happen and how will you know it? The answer is: it's not important. The best way to listen to a movement in sonata form is exactly the same way that you watch a movie or a play. You follow the story from one moment to the next, taking in each event as it happens. If you know the music well in advance, the surprises inevitably become less surprising, but you will become naturally more conscious of both interesting details and deeper expressive nuances.

Another reason you don't need to worry about what section you are in or what subject you are hearing is that any movement in sonata form is going to spend much of its time not in presenting its themes but in actually moving from one place (key) to the next. In fact, it would be just as accurate to describe a sonata-form movement as containing two contrasting kinds of music:

the tunes and motives that give a feeling of being in a specific key or location, and the transitional ideas (often highly rhythmic and vigorous in quick music, and harmonically rich and interesting in slow) that signal "action" and advance the musical argument.

If you want to hear a couple of examples of this sort of "action music," listen to the first movement of the "Jupiter" Symphony, CD track 1 at 0:13, and the first movement of the G Minor Symphony, CD track 2 at 0:30. The excitement and forward drive of these two passages speak for themselves, but not all such examples (particularly in chamber music) are so vigorous. It is also possible, for example, to use long *transition themes,* or passages of rapidly shifting harmony, to achieve the same ends, as for example Mozart does in the first movement of his G Minor String Quintet (CD track 6 at 0:32). In this case, strange and dissonant harmony clouds the listener's feeling of being in the home key, and Mozart resolves this tension when the second subject appears a few second later. So there are actually just as many options in writing transitions as there are in coming up with the ideas comprising the first and second subjects.

For this reason, it works better when listening if you don't think of sonata form as a movement in three sections at all but rather consider it as a *process* that needs to be followed as it unfolds in time. If understanding the process requires recollection of an important theme or motive, then Mozart will ensure that you do, but for the most part much of the satisfaction inherent in sonata form resides in your unconscious feeling of being either "home," "away," or "in transit." You don't have to be able to identify what key you are in, or even know what *key* means, in order to grasp the music's expressive intentions. No matter how intellectually erudite a sonata movement may be, it requires little if any comparable sophistication on the part of the listener.

This reality stands in stark opposition to the commonly held myth that the classical style, and Mozart's in particular, is complex, because audiences in the eighteenth century were musically more experienced than audiences today. Even if correct, it does not logically follow that the forms of classical music (and of sonata style in particular) have to be uniquely complicated just because they were written for such an audience. Musical training is no guarantor of intelligence, and musical form arises from the simple truth that there are only so many ways to organize a large piece in several movements so that it doesn't bore a listener to death. When you think about it, sonata form could never have become so ubiquitous, and its greatest examples the most popular classics of the past 250 years or so, if it catered only to the most exalted tastes of a particular time and place. Common sense suggests just the opposite. So does the expressive power of Mozart's music.

Conclusion: A Practical Example

I don't really have to summarize the above discussion in words, because Mozart has done it in music. You can actually hear the entire contents of this chapter explained to you in far more charming fashion than I can possibly manage verbally if, in addition to the sample selections already mentioned, you spend some time listening to:

Divertimento in E-flat, K. 563, for string trio (1788)

This remarkable work for violin, viola, and cello offers an ideal illustration of all the formal types and tendencies just discussed. A *divertimento* means the same thing as a *serenade, cassation, notturno,* or *partita:* that is, a multi-movement work intended specifically for light entertainment. Mozart wrote a lot of them, and you will encounter several in the upcoming sections of this book. The way to make a large piece of music less intellectually demanding in Mozart's day was not, as you might expect, to make it shorter. Just the opposite: works of this type often add extra movements, although in less challenging forms, such as minuets and rondos, and may even (in orchestral music) include entire mini-concertos or concerto movements featuring a particular soloist.

However, by the time he came to write K. 563, Mozart was so far beyond caring about the distinction between "light" and "serious" music, preferring instead to be both great and entertaining at one and the same time, that the result in this case is incomparably the largest and grandest work in existence for string trio. In fact, although it isn't known for sure, it seems that the most plausible reason Mozart wrote those extra movements and made this piece so big was simply because he relished the challenge of finding as much variety as possible within this particularly rigorous medium. One thing you'll come to understand very quickly about Mozart as you listen is that the more compositional difficulties he sets for himself, the more impressive his success is likely to be.

The divertimento's six movements, which together last about forty-five minutes in performance (depending on the treatment of repeats), are arranged as follows:

1. Allegro (fast)—sonata form: The first phrase of the second subject might be a Mozartean paraphrase of "Hot Time in the Old Town Tonight" (sadly, a chronological impossibility).
2. Adagio (slow): sonata form.
3. Minuet: allegretto (a little fast)—ABA.
4. Andante (walking tempo): theme and four variations (all of them "double," with the third variation wonderfully brooding in a somber minor key).

5. Minuet: allegretto again, although simpler in rhythm and more rustic in mood than the first minuet, and this time with two trio sections producing a basic rondo form—ABACA.

6. Allegro (fast): sonata-rondo hybrid (In other words, A is the first subject and B is the second subject. A returns before the development—which constitutes C—and also at the very end to round off the form in typical rondo fashion).

In addition to displaying almost every major formal type available to Mozart in his day, the fact that only three solo string players participate means that the music will tend naturally to involve a great deal of contrapuntal interplay, while the complete absence of harmonic "filler" means that passages of simply accompanied melody contrast boldly with those in three equal voices. You can hear this particularly clearly in the finale (which has an opening tune so catchy you'll swear you've heard it before) and in the andante's variations, but the alternation of homophonic and polyphonic passages is a major organizing principal behind the entire work no matter what particular form an individual movement happens to adopt. So here it is: the entire gamut of classical form and style in one very convenient package.

The next chapter, where I look systematically at all the music on the accompanying CD, will give you a lot more information about the way Mozart uses these formal types and will allow you actually to hear his personal stylistic fingerprints, but I have placed this wonderful piece here for several reasons aside from its sheer formal variety. First, it stands outside of the standard canon of Mozart's most popular efforts as a sort of "one-shot wonder" that deserves to be far better known. Second, some readers may savor the opportunity of listening to a sample of Mozart's best production without further explanation, coming to it fresh as did music lovers in his own time and letting its newness speak for itself. Third, no discussions of musical form and style approach in value the time you are willing spend listening. Finally and most importantly, the tunes are gorgeous (that second subject of the adagio with those wide leaps in the violin—wow!), and after all this discussion of form, the bottom line is that if you don't like the melodies, then you certainly aren't going to care about how Mozart arranges them, right? So why wait and why worry? Just jump right in and enjoy.

What Makes Mozart Sound Like Mozart?

In the preceding chapter, I noted some of the personal touches that characterize Mozart's use of form, but frankly these pale beside the traits that distinguish the music that those forms contain. What makes Mozart so special? There's a simple answer and a more complex one. Simply put, he is the first composer in history known principally as a writer of great tunes. While other composers before him turned out some very famous ones too (Bach, Handel, Vivaldi, and Haydn, to name just four, were certainly no slouches in that department), with all due respect for their achievements, none of their reputations rest on the sheer gorgeousness of the melodies that they created to the same degree that Mozart's does.

Unfortunately, describing what makes a melody "gorgeous," or at least personal to the extent that it sounds like no one else, tests the very limits of what one can do with words alone. So let's have both a look and a listen to some examples of the six most important and distinctly audible qualities that give Mozart's melodies their particular flavor, with most of the examples tied to the music on the accompanying compact disc.

I. The Vocal Foundation of Mozart's Music

Any composer whose fame rests largely on tunes understands that all musical instruments exist to imitate or accompany, in one way or another, the human voice. The sheer "singability" of Mozart's music, whether vocal or instrumental, is one of its most noteworthy qualities. Mozart understood the capabilities of the voice as have few others, even famous opera composers, and singers will tell you that his music is always grateful, even healthy, to sing. These same vocal qualities carry over to his instrumental music as well, only heightened and intensified to compensate for, and take advantage of, the lack of an actual text.

To see how this works in reality, you will find on track 7 of the accompanying CD a tiny aria that Mozart composed for insertion in another composer's opera at the request of a lead singer. I offer the first two sentences of text (there are a couple more, all in the same vein, so there's no need to quote them). When you listen to this aria, pay special attention to the music at the words "Voi siete un po'tondo." This music and text will return to conclude the aria (or *arietta* as Mozart called it), so you get to hear them twice, and they are accompanied by a sprightly march that neatly illustrates the suggestion to "go out and study the ways of the world." This arietta is all of two minutes long, so you may want to listen a few times to get that tune into your head.

"Un bacio di mano," K. 541

Un bacio di mano	A kiss on the hand
Vi fa maraviglia,	Will accomplish wonders for you.
E poi bella figlia,	And now, lovely girl,
Volete sposar.	You are ready to get married.
Voi siete un po'tondo,	You're a little foolish,
Mio caro Pompeo,	My dear Pompeo.

L'usanze del mondo	Go out and study
Andate a studiar.	The ways of the world.

Now turn to track 1 of the CD, where you will find the first movement of Mozart's Symphony No. 41 ("Jupiter"). Composed shortly after this aria, its second subject includes the same tune at 2:33, played by the violins, later joined by woodwinds. If we compare the two versions of this melody, we discover that:

- In the symphony, the tune is not played to the accompaniment of a march. This is because the symphony's very opening is in march tempo, and Mozart wants contrast, not more of the same.
- The tempo in the symphony is quicker.
- Mozart retains the shape of the melody, including the repeated notes and the natural stress of the words.

All this enhances, rather than reduces, the melody's conversational quality. Instead of words to amuse us, we have the chattering violins that give us their expressive sense—their dry wit. This quality of instruments, not just breaking into song but playing a song so word-specific that they often seem trembling on the verge of actual speech, helps give Mozart's melodies their ability to communicate human emotion so directly. As you can hear, he achieves this by making the instruments imitate (often through exaggeration of tempo, rhythm, repeated notes, or range) the typical things that voices do when singing and speaking. In short, Mozart's instrumental writing is "spiced up" vocal music, and you would be perfectly justified in making up words of your own to many of the tunes that otherwise lack them. Surely Mozart himself did just that, and one can only imagine what amusing inside jokes he must have shared within his circle of friends whenever they heard certain particularly catchy tunes.

To make this example even clearer, turn to track 11 on your sample CD, the overture to the opera *Don Giovanni*. This overture begins with a slow introduction illustrating a supernatural event from the opera's last act: the horrifying appearance of the animated statue of the murdered Commendatore, come to consign the Don to the flames of hell. Eventually, at 1:50, this vision yields to the quick music of the opera's comic elements, but the important point is that until he reaches the main body of the movement, Mozart writes not a single tune. The music is all texture and pattern without extended melody. By eliminating the vocal element (and the humanity that it conveys), this introduction becomes a portrayal of supernatural terror. It is, in fact, what one would call today "horror movie" scoring—pure atmosphere—and its effect is chilling.

These three examples neatly sum up one of the fundamental facts concerning instrumental music that all composers face in creating their personal styles. When instruments are used in imitation of voices, they express human feelings. A listener, on hearing a specific tune, intuitively identifies with and understands its vocal basis and imaginatively supplies, if not actual words, then their more abstract emotional meaning. On the other hand, when instruments are used in ways that ignore this melodic or vocal element, the music instead either creates a certain atmosphere and mood or describes nonhuman objects—be they storms, sunrises, birds, outer space, the sea, trains, or whatever else catches the composer's fancy and fires his imagination. Mozart, though, takes the technique of writing instrumental "vocal" music to heights of refinement and virtuosity unequalled either before or since.

2. Melodic Shapes in Fast Movements

There are almost an infinite number of ways to write tunes, but Mozart in his quick music shows a distinct preference for certain melodic shapes. He shares this characteristic with other composers of his day, and some of these patterns constitute the stock in trade of the classical style, but as in all such cases, a great composer makes these patterns very much his own. Here are four:

The "Question and Answer"

You can hear this at the very opening of track 1 on the CD. The "Jupiter" Symphony opens with a loud statement followed by a gently feminine answer, stated twice. The finale of Symphony No. 40, K. 550, turns this idea on its head: a gentle question produces a robust answer.

The "Arch"

This type of tune generally begins with a rising phrase followed by a falling one. The opening of the above-mentioned Symphony No. 40 (CD track 2) is one example, and so is the opening phrase of the G Minor String Quintet (CD track 6). The first half of the main theme of the finale of Piano Concerto No. 17 (CD track 4) offers a particularly expansive case of this technique, but perhaps the most famous example is the string flourish that opens *Eine Kleine Nachtmusik*.

The "Mosaic"

Just as artists build large mosaics from little bits and pieces of material, so composers can construct longer melodies or even large musical tracts from the repetition of smaller motives, whether highly distinctive in shape and color or relatively neutral. The second subject of the G Minor String Quintet's first movement (CD track 6 at 0:55) offers a prime example: a four-note motive dominates large tracts of music both here and later in the development section (at 6:30). You may also want to return to the opening of Symphony No. 40 (CD track 2) and pay special attention to the descending three-note figure out of which Mozart builds both the first subject and the end of the second subject (at 1:18).

Similarly, the opening movement of the "Jupiter" Symphony (CD track 1) builds itself up from a series of bold but intentionally foursquare and somewhat impersonal gestures, rhythms, and textures—at least until one gets to the actual tune in the second subject described above. I need to clarify one point here: when I say a movement has "no tunes" or is "built from commonplace elements," the extent to which you recognize this will necessarily depend on your familiarity with the classical style.

Indeed on first hearing, such a movement's ideas may sound quite original because they are new to you personally, but the more you listen, the more you will note the resemblances to other works and to common habits of the musical idiom of the period. Over time, the unique character of the themes will strike you less and the movement's large-scale shape and structure impress you more. Your vision of the music will naturally change over time, just as your perception of a pointillist painting varies depending on whether you see it up close, as patterns of tiny colored dots, or from afar as a composition consisting of larger shapes and images. Nor does the fact that a movement may be built from "ready-made" themes or simple motives mean that they are in any way unappealing or dull.

The "Nursery Rhyme"

In the preceding survey of form, I noted that often the subjects of variations or rondo finales are very catchy, simple tunes of childlike simplicity. Mozart writes them this way because he wants their basic figures to be instantly recognizable and memorable. Your CD contains two examples of this very frequently occurring habit, one a set of variations, one a rondo, both finales. The first example is the variation finale of Piano Concerto No. 17 (CD track 4). I have no doubt that you will be able to hum this tune after hearing it for the very first time. The finale of the "Gran Partita" for thirteen wind instruments (CD track 10) is a very fast rondo, so the tune may be more difficult to sing at the proper speed, but it's no less catchy and identifiable whenever it returns.

All this repetition and symmetry may lead you to think that Mozart's melodic thinking is dull and regular, but nothing could be further from the truth. Quite often the entire point of these regular shapes is to provide a contrast with the surprising continuations, unexpected twists, and suspenseful turns that Mozart holds in reserve. Sometimes, though, the music's sheer high spirits leads Mozart to abandon any pretense of symmetry and let the music appear to trip over itself with cartoonlike glee. So as a suggestion for further listening, I leave you with two of the happiest examples of this very special type of quick melody, in the form of the overture to the opera *The Marriage of Figaro* and the finale of Symphony No. 35 ("Haffner").

3. Slow Melodies

Mozart's slow movements, whatever their form, all share an exceptional graciousness and melodic beauty, so much so that they have become the paradigm of the "perfect" lyrical classical style. One of the things that makes them so special is Mozart's ability to spin out a long melody that, while actually highly organized in structure, gives the impression of a passage of endless, improvised song. The first example in his work of this compositional gift (no other word really explains it) is probably the slow movement of the Violin Concerto No. 3, K. 216, where the gently caressing strings and sighing flutes create a breathtaking backdrop against which the soloist plays a positively heavenly melody.

Undoubtedly the most famous tune of this type belongs to the slow movement of Piano Concerto No. 21, K. 467. This is the theme that appeared in the Swedish film *Elvira Madigan* and so gave the entire concerto a nickname as confusing as any, since virtually no one has seen the movie, and the only thing that perpetuates its name is Mozart's concerto and not the other way around. But then, a tune this beautiful defies logic anyway, and you can enjoy it on CD track 3. The form is basically ABA. Violins announce the melody over a throbbing accompaniment that persists uninterrupted for almost the entire movement. The piano takes up the theme (at 1:40) and interpolates a soulful, minor-key episode before coming back to its closing phrases. A short middle section (beginning at 4:00) leads back to the original tune on the piano (at 5:17), but you may notice that Mozart saves its middle phrase for use at the very end.

There are more formal subtleties here that you can discover at your leisure, but there's no need to go into them any further when the entire point of the music is to give the impression of a single, endless melody. The contrast between a movement such as this—a sustained passage of song more than six minutes long—and the short-winded efforts of so many of Mozart's lesser contemporaries is truly remarkable. If you take my word for it on this last issue, you not only get to enjoy this hypnotically seductive movement, you also save yourself the trouble of wading through the short-winded efforts of Mozart's lesser contemporaries.

4. Instrumental Colors and Wonderful Woodwinds

The most naturally "vocal" of all instrumental families is the woodwind group: flutes, oboes, clarinets, and bassoons. The reason for this is simple: these instruments rely for sound production on a column of air passing over a vibrating reed, just as the voice depends on a column of air passing over vibrating vocal chords. The natural determinate of phrasing for both voices and woodwind instruments is the limit of a single human breath, unlike strings or keyboards, which can sustain long musical passages without pause and play multiple notes simultaneously. Mozart demanded the largest possible complement of woodwind instruments at every opportunity, nowhere more so than in what remains the greatest work ever written for this particular family, the "Gran Partita," K. 361/370a (also known as Serenade No. 10), for thirteen wind instruments: two oboes, two bassoons, two clarinets, two basset horns (ancestors of the bass clarinet), four horns, and contrabassoon (or double bass). You can hear the finale of this extraordinary work on CD track 10.

If woodwinds are the closest of all instrumental families to the human voice, then the clarinet is the most vocal of all wind instruments. Like the voice, it has three distinct registers: a piercing upper range, a mellow middle, and a throaty "chest" (called *chalumeau* in clarinet jargon). In Mozart's day the clarinet was a novelty, just beginning to make its way into symphonic and wind ensemble music, and fortunately for posterity, Mozart became good friends with the Stadler brothers, the greatest clarinetists of their day. It is to them in particular that we owe the existence of one of Mozart's last works, the Clarinet Concerto, K. 622, as well as the very famous Clarinet Quintet, K. 581, the first movement of which you can hear on CD track 5.

Mozart's love affair with the clarinet is not limited to those works that feature it as a solo instrument. He used pairs of clarinets wherever possible in the orchestration of his operas, concertos, and symphonies. In his Symphony No. 39, he dispenses with oboes entirely so as to color the entire work with the more mellow and vocally expressive tone of the clarinet, and the trio of that work's minuet (CD track 9 at 2:03) offers the two players an opportunity to make this fact especially clear. Mozart even went through the trouble of rewriting the woodwind parts of his Symphony No. 40, originally conceived without clarinets, to include a pair of them, as soon as he knew that they would be available for a subsequent performance.

There's another, equally important reason that Mozart loved to combine as many different kinds of instrumental color as possible, particularly in his orchestral works. In chamber music, where each player maintains his identity as a soloist, the risk is minimal of losing the kind of personal expressiveness that Mozart's melodies require. Orchestras, though, being larger and necessarily requiring numerous players on each musical line (particularly true of the strings), cannot phrase and inflect a tune the way an instrumental or vocal soloist can, and this can make the music sound stiff, mechanical, and lacking in character. Mozart compensates for this, constantly varying the color of his orchestral melodies by shifting them from one instrumental family to another, repeating them in a way that always presents them in a fresh light. The free use of his highly vocal woodwind section is the logical outcome of this desire for maximum expressiveness in an orchestral context.

To hear how this works, listen closely to the finale of Piano Concerto No. 17 (CD track 4). This is, as mentioned previously, a "theme and variations," one in which Mozart has the additional advantage of creating contrast by using the piano soloist in addition to the full orchestra, which here consists of a single flute;

pairs of oboes, bassoons, and horns; plus the usual strings (violins, violas, cellos, and basses). So the orchestra isn't at all large, but listen to what an amazing amount of color and variety Mozart squeezes out of this modest ensemble!

Theme: As noted previously, the subject of the variations is a nursery-rhyme type of melody in two halves, both repeated, with the full wind section adding a witty commentary to the last notes of each phrase.

Variation 1 (at 0:47): Also in two halves, both repeated literally, this belongs to the piano accompanied lightly by the strings.

Variation 2 (at 1:34): From this point on, all the variations are double, meaning that the repeats are themselves varied. The first half of the theme is played by the full wind section against a running accompaniment in the piano's upper register. Its repeat features the theme in the strings and the pianist's right hand against the same running accompaniment in the piano's low register. The second half of the theme follows this pattern.

Variation 3 (at 2:20): Each of the winds in turn (oboe, flute, bassoon) has a brief solo, while the repeat of the theme's first half goes to the piano. The second half of the variation, where the original melody is much clearer, repeats this pattern, with the winds entering in the order: flute, bassoon, and then oboe.

Variation 4 (at 3:14): You won't hear the melody at all in this variation, which is a solemn meditation in a dark minor key. The first half of the theme belongs to the strings inflected by gentle woodwind colors above, and the repeat is a piano solo with no instrumental accompaniment at all. The second half of the theme repeats the pattern of the first half, except that when the solo piano takes over on the repeat, the woodwinds interject a few bars of anguished commentary as well.

Variation 5 (at 4:11): This is a battle between the full orchestra on each half of the theme's initial statement and the unaccompanied solo piano that has a much clearer version of the original tune on the repeat.

Coda: A witty transition follows the fifth variation, with the solo-ist seeming not to know quite where it's going, finally coming to a full stop. Then the music takes off in a dazzling coda based on an entirely new theme (at 5:30). Strings begin, winds add their voices, and when the soloist finally reenters (at 5:48) he or she is accompanied by the wind section alone. Shortly afterwards, the variation theme shows up briefly in the new, very fast tempo (at 6:33), and the rest of the movement is all brilliant windup.

5. Rhythm

In the introduction, I noted that Mozart's music seldom engages in description of anything other than human activities: marching, dancing, hunting, and so forth. Each of these activities, when represented musically, has traditional rhythmic associations, and when it comes to dance music and march music especially, Mozart brands each type with his own special personality.

Minuets

The minuet is a dance in 3/4 time, like the waltz, having a basic rhythm in each bar of: *one,* two, three (that is, the accent falls on the first beat). Mozart's minuets, of which that of Symphony No. 39 (CD track 9) furnishes a typical example, reveal his love of long-breathed melodies, even in this normally short-winded context. They tend to move at a moderate tempo (many of his contemporaries wrote faster ones), and their tunes are usually stately and graceful. Mozart seldom hammers home the underlying rhythm of a minuet in the way that Haydn and Beethoven love to do: his music glides more than it stomps, and he's always willing to break the basic rhythm through syncopation or asymmetrical melodies in order to sustain the listener's interest.

In this respect, it's important to note the distinction between real dance music, of which Mozart composed a great deal for Viennese court balls (some of it is marvelous) and the pieces that Mozart intended for insertion into large symphonic and chamber works. As mentioned in discussing vocal music, Mozart heightens the music's basic elements in this abstract instrumental context though exaggeration: these pieces are bigger, longer, grander, more colorful, and melodically more captivating than music written as mere accompaniment to the physical activity of dancing. Indeed, some of Mozart's minuets, particularly in chamber works such as the String Quartet No. 14, K. 387, or the String Quintet in C major, K. 515, are truly huge and chock-full of variety: longer in duration than the slow movements or finales of the same works. They remain the largest examples of the minuet in existence, for this dance was soon replaced (thanks to Haydn and Beethoven) by the generally much faster and more boisterous instrumental movement known as the *scherzo*.

Marches

Music that is not is some form of triple-time dance rhythm and that is not moving at a very high rate of speed generally falls into march tempo, either fast or slow. Virtually all great composers wrote marches, but very few display a personal "march style." Beethoven and Mahler had one, and so did Mozart. Indeed, so frequently does Mozart stylize music of a marchlike or military character in his works that he appropriated a specific rhythm that serves almost as his musical fingerprint. You can hear this very simple rhythm at the opening of the "Jupiter" Symphony after the initial sequence of questions and answers (CD track 1 at 0:13). The rhythm goes like this: *dum, dum, dadum,* and it might be represented in the natural cadences of speech by the exclamation "Mozart arrives!" His use of it is too frequent and widespread to require further comment here. You'll find this rhythm particularly prominent in orchestral works where Mozart uses trumpets and timpani.

Syncopation and Palpitation

Much of the rhythmic interest in the music of any great composer of melodies belongs in their accompaniments. Mozart developed countless ways of "floating" a melody atop a huge variety of rhythmic shapes. Two are of particular concern. The first is what might be called a "palpitation"—a sort of regular pulsation like a beating heart that can sometimes run almost through an entire movement. The famous andante of Piano Concerto No. 21 (CD track 3) provides one extremely vivid example. This technique works in quicker tempos too: witness the opening movement of the String Quintet, K. 516, with both first (CD track 6) and second (at 0:55) subjects accompanied by a steady pattern of repeated notes. These simple rhythmic figures not only energize the music by providing a sense of forward motion, they also increase the vertical tension by pulling against the principal melodies that they accompany, particularly (as in the case of the piano concerto and the quintet's second subject) when the melodies themselves include wide-spanning phrases in long notes.

Mozart increases this melodic tension still further by his use of syncopation: having the accompaniment played "off the beat."

The introduction to the overture from *Don Giovanni* derives much of its unsettling quality from this device, and you can hear exactly the same technique at the equally threatening opening of the Piano Concerto No. 20, both of which happen to be in the same "sad" key of D Minor. However, perhaps the easiest way to hear clearly the wonderful expressiveness that Mozart obtains through syncopation under a melody is to listen to the second subject of the Clarinet Quintet's first movement (CD track 5). First it's played in a major key by solo violin over immobile, sustained chords, then immediately followed (at 1:40) in a minor key by solo clarinet over a syncopated accompaniment in the string quartet. The impression of wistful anxiety that this contrast conveys really is indescribable in words.

6. Harmony

Harmony and its associated concepts of key and tonality are the most difficult musical qualities to describe in words, first because they have no true analogues in other art forms, and second because the expressive meaning of various chords and keys is subjective, differing from person to person. So attempts to describe the harmonic aspects of a given piece of music (especially when it comes to movements organized around a particular tonal scheme, such as those in sonata form) often wind up being either highly technical and virtually incomprehensible, or poetically descriptive but basically meaningless. Without minimizing the difficulty of addressing this issue, particularly with respect to composers such as Mozart, whose sophistication in matters of tonality and harmony was second to none, it's certainly possible to selectively point out specific examples of his special way with harmony and tonality that are easy to hear and understand. Only two aspects of Mozart's use of harmony and tonality in the presentation of his melodies concern the listener in any case: mode and chromatics.

Mode

In our tonal system, the twelve possible keys each have two modes: major and minor. Major keys generally express feelings of happiness, joy, and contentment, while minor ones depict anger, sadness, and lamentation. Even when music describes natural objects or events, what it really does is express the emotional qualities of the thing being described. Thus, most musical sunrises are happy and stick to major keys, while most storms are angry and violent and so employ the minor. These are universal constants in our musical tradition, and while opinions may vary as to the intensity of emotion being expressed (is it wistful sadness or breast-beating despair?), the major/happy, minor/sad antithesis enjoys general acceptance among composers, scholars, and listeners everywhere.

Now this is all nice to know, but the problem arises in trying to describe what a minor key sounds like as opposed to a major one. The only thing one can do is point out examples of each and let listeners draw their own conclusions. Happily, Mozart's music is full of contrast between major and minor keys, often in very close proximity so that you can hear the difference quite clearly. The overture to *Don Giovanni* (CD track 11), for example, opens with the most intense minor-key music that Mozart ever wrote, followed by a zippy major-key allegro (at 1:50). Note that Mozart seldom asks you to hear the contrast in isolation: he highlights the change of mode by also changing tempo, instrumentation, and theme: in other words, changes in mode work in association with all the other qualities of color and contrast discussed so far.

One of the most powerful uses of the contrast between major and minor mode is to repeat a melody, moving from one mode to the other. If you've been listening to the examples already presented, then you already know what this sounds like. The second subject of the Clarinet Quintet's first movement (CD track 5) does just that, playing the tune first in the major (at 1:25) and then in the minor when the clarinet has it a few seconds later (at 1:40). As the melody works its way quickly back to the major mode (at 1:58), the effect is like a cloud passing in front of the sun. The full implications of the excursion into the minor don't become obvious until recapitulation, when (at 8:00) the clarinet refuses to let go of the minor mode and so creates a dramatic crisis—more on this shortly.

Mozart's music is full of such minor key "excursions." The great outburst in the "Jupiter" Symphony's first movement (CD track 1 at 2:04) offers another example, and indeed these are so common that it's probably fair to say that no great work of Mozart goes without one for long. This mixing of modes is as much a part of his expressive arsenal as the mixing of instrumental colors. Recall, for example, the impressive minor-key variation in the finale of Piano Concerto No. 17 (CD track 4 at 3:14). Even so, organizing entire works around minor keys was extremely unusual in Mozart's day, and only a handful of his works boast this distinction: two symphonies, two piano concertos, and a tiny sampling of chamber music. Because of their rarity as well as their emotional intensity, these pieces stand among Mozart's most famous. Two of them are represented by their first movements on the accompanying CD: Symphony No. 40 in G Minor (CD track 2) and the String Quintet in G Minor, K. 516 (CD track 6).

Chromatics

Another special harmonic feature of Mozart's style is his frequent use of chromaticism. This is actually quite easy to understand as soon as you know what it is. When you hear it said that melody or harmony is *chromatic* (the term means "colored"), all it means is that the tune (or chord) uses notes (or chords) foreign to the music's basic key. This is possible because out of twelve equally spaced notes in a full (or chromatic) scale, only seven define the major or minor modes of any given key. As you may well imagine, the presence of these "aliens" upsets the sense of being firmly in a given key and increases the amount of dissonance (that is, harmonic tension arising from notes that clash when played together). Extensive passages of chromaticism produce the musical equivalent of driving into a dense fog without knowing exactly where you will come out again, and so serve the dramatic aspects of the sonata style particularly well.

Used sparingly, chromaticism spices up the expressive character of the melody in question, and Mozart most often uses it for just this purpose. In association with minor keys, chromaticism often enhances a melody's pathetic or despairing character. For example, the opening phrase of the G Minor String Quintet's first subject (CD track 6) consists of two six-note motives, and the second of these is a descending chromatic scale that greatly increases the music's nervous anxiety. Later in the movement (at 0:32), Mozart uses a passage of chromatic harmony to obliterate the listener's sense of key and so prepare for the surprise of the introduction of the second subject—unusually, still in G Minor—that only gradually evolves into its "proper" key. The use of chromatic harmony here both enlarges the form and heightens the exposition's intensity, by leading listeners to believe that they were "going somewhere" when in fact Mozart had no such intention quite yet. The movement also concludes with a wonderfully dark coda featuring this same new theme, decorated by slithering chromatic scales (at 10:56).

It would be a mistake, however, to assume that the effectiveness of this "chromatic spice" is limited to the expression of sadness. Far from it! When used to flavor major keys, chromaticism can actually increase the music's sense of fun and good humor. In the finale of the "Gran Partita" (CD track 10), Mozart twice interrupts the "big finish" with a descending chromatic scale that has the effect of sucking the wind right out of the music's sails. The effect only serves to emphasize by contrast the high spirits of the ending when it ultimately arrives. A similar descending chromatic scale towards the end of the Clarinet Quintet's first movement (CD track 5 at 9:14) serves much the same purpose, affirming rather than undermining the smile with which the music concludes.

In the hands of more than a few later composers, the use of chromaticism became an expressive cliché, particularly because in the romantic period the use of tonality as the work's prime structural element gradually declined. Because Mozart's forms are so clear and his use of harsh dissonance is so sparing, he extracts the maximum expressive effect from the minimum amount of chromatic decoration. Like all great chefs, musical or otherwise, he never ruins high-quality ingredients by smothering them in an excess of seasoning.

7. Wit and Pathos

I have so far examined some of the techniques and strategies that Mozart employs to give his music its special character, but the question still remains: what makes it uniquely expressive? It can be taken for granted that all great composers write music that runs the gamut of emotions from joy to despair, but the classical style as perfected by Mozart widened this range to include both humor and pathos. These qualities seldom if ever characterize the music of earlier epochs, largely because (as you may have surmised from the above discussion) both rely to some extent on the contrasts made possible by the the sonata style.

Wit

Of these two characteristics, wit is the more difficult to define, because no two people have the same sense of humor (assuming that they have one at all) and because the pretensions of so-called serious artists playing serious music—not to mention the cultural afflatus surrounding the modern experience of the "classics"— aren't exactly conducive to laughter. Things were very different in Mozart's day, when there was no perceived conflict between music's quality and its value simply as a superior form of light and diverting entertainment.

Nevertheless, the fact remains that much of Mozart's music is very witty. Unlike Haydn, from whom he learned a lot about music's humorous potential, and despite the fact that he wrote a piece called *A Musical Joke,* Mozart's humor is not often of the laugh-out-loud, slapstick variety. Rather, as with all of his expressive devices, it is a function of his music's vocal qualities: the wit lies primarily in the unfolding instrumental dialogue. Because of its vocal nature, it often can be found particularly vividly in Mozart's treatment of woodwind instruments. The opening of the finale of Piano Concerto No. 17, for example (CD track 4), is an amusing tune on its face (as are most such nursery-rhyme themes) by virtue of its very simplicity, but the woodwind chuckles at the end of each phrase deepen and reinforce the music's humor. The very fast coda (at 5:30), and especially the speeded-up appearance of the variation theme, only confirms this witty impression.

In the discussion of chromaticism, I noted the humorous effect of descending chromatic scales in the finale of the "Gran Partita" (CD track 10), but this entire rondo gives the impression of almost cartoonish fun, thanks to the fruity timbres of the wind instruments and the dashing cut of Mozart's themes. The quiet restatement of the "Jupiter" Symphony's question-and-answer first subject (CD track 1 at 0:38) finds itself accompanied by chuckling flutes that make light of the theme's pomposity on its first appearance, while at the very beginning of this discussion, I noted the witty character of the second subject, taken from the aria "Un bacio di mano" (at 2:33), where the instrumental setting actually enhances the humorous sense of the text. This sort of conversational wit, based on the give-and-take of ongoing instrumental dialogue, has few real parallels in the music of other composers, save that of Haydn, who basically invented the technique in his String Quartets, Op. 33.

Pathos

Just as Dante's *Inferno* gets much more attention than his *Paradiso,* so misery in music tends to be far more highly respected and acclaimed than humor. In the first place, unhappy music strikes most listeners as more "serious" and "deep" than joyous music. It's also easier to write (as it seldom risks generalized blandness) and easier for audiences to recognize, particularly when (as in the case of Mozart) the infrequency and special quality of music in minor (unhappy) keys automatically marks it as something out of the ordinary. But pathos, like wit, is a very specific quality that Mozart happens to be so good at that everyone agrees he's the master, even if most people aren't exactly sure what it means. I would define it in Mozartean terms as sadness without despair, or the expression of suffering devoid of misery or self-pity.

Mozart creates pathos in one of three ways. The first is to simply write a tune that conveys this particular quality, such as the opening of Symphony No. 40 (CD track 2) or the G Minor String Quintet (CD track 6). The second method involves repeating a melody in a major key and immediately following it with a minor-key variant, as heard in the second subject of the first movement of the Clarinet Quintet (CD track 5 at 1:40). This gives the music a bittersweet quality and deepens its mood, even if the major key ultimately prevails.

Finally, as mentioned in the discussion of sonata form, in works based on minor keys, Mozart likes to keep his second subjects in the tonic minor even when tradition suggests he should provide a major-key or happy ending. He does this both in the first movement of the G Minor String Quintet (CD track 6) and Symphony No. 40 (CD track 2). The effect is similar to what happens in the Clarinet Quintet, only on a larger scale. In order to appreciate this device, you have to listen to the entire movement so as to hear it in context, but for a good example, compare what happens to the second subject in the symphony (at 0:47 and 5:52).

Conclusion: The Big Picture

The seven elements just discussed may or may not appear in each mature work by Mozart, but some of them invariably do. Most of them are related both to each other and to the general vocal character of Mozart's instrumental music. In order to offer a sense of how they all come together to create the inimitable musical style that we recognize as Mozart's—and Mozart's alone—let's spend about nine minutes looking at an entire movement in detail, in this case the first movement of the Clarinet Quintet (CD track 5). Some of the points in the following description have already been made, but I still think it's important to place them in the context of the actual music when viewed as a whole rather than considering them in isolation, however useful that may be initially.

Mozart scores the quintet for clarinet and string quartet (that is, two violins, viola, and cello). The first movement is in spectacularly clear sonata form.

First Subject

The first subject consists of a string quartet question followed by a clarinet answer, both of which are immediately repeated. Strictly speaking, this is the entire first subject. Violin and viola immediately take up the clarinet's answer (at 0:33), and from this point on, the music consists of transitional material—that is, a passage designed to give the impression of movement from the home key to that of the second subject.

Mozart achieves this impression by introducing a new theme on the clarinet (at 0:37), foreshortened and repeated by the cello, then further abbreviated on the violin, and finally turning into a dialogue between clarinet and violin (at 1:10), with the violin turning the clarinet's phrases upside down. This continual shortening of the musical phrases gives the impression of increasing speed and energy, and Mozart heightens the impression by moving from an accompaniment of sustained chords (at 0:37) to one of repeated notes (at 1:01), finally arriving at a climax and full stop.

I describe this transition fully because, as I mentioned in the discussion of sonata form, much of the material in a movement of this type moves the music from one key to the next and actually takes more time than the formally designated first or second subjects. It often provides material for the development section and may even contain the most memorable tunes, so when listening, as I suggested in the last chapter, it's usually more important to get a feel for the contrast between periods of "motion" and "rest" than it is to be able to say for certain exactly what tune belongs to what section of the movement.

Second Subject

At 1:25, the first violin begins the haunting tune of the famous second subject, and we have already seen how the clarinet continues it in a minor key under a syncopated rhythmic accompaniment. As the harmony veers back towards the major, the rhythm once again becomes more active, and the music reaches a climax capped by a trill in the violins and clarinet (at 2:11). Next follows a cadence theme (a tune designed to "close off" the exposition), in exactly the same question-and-answer format as the first subject, although the tune is different. Mozart then returns to the first subject and, in a witty gesture, has the clarinet interrupt the question with the second (faster) half of the answer. Three sharp chords bring the exposition to a firm close. Most performances (including this one) repeat the exposition from the beginning as Mozart directs.

Development

Beginning at 5:29 with an upward chromatic run in the clarinet, we return to the first subject, but when the answer arrives, it's played by each of the strings in turn, starting from the top down. This quickly turns into a vigorous episode, in which each of the strings takes turns playing figures derived from the fast second half of the answer, while the clarinet strides up and down, outlining the harmony of each new chord as it's sustained by the remaining strings. This is, once again, "motion music," and as it settles down to statements of the full answer (at 6:29), this time from the bottom up—starting with the viola—it leads swiftly back to the first subject.

Recapitulation (at 6:44)

Although the music is basically the same as at the beginning, Mozart scores it differently. The clarinet now participates in the question, the first violin has the answer, and Mozart omits the repetition of both, moving straight to the transitional material, which sounds pretty much as previously. The second subject sails in (at 7:45) on the first violin as expected, but when the clarinet takes it up (at 8:00), something wonderful happens. It plays a free variation of the tune, and instead of swiftly reclaiming the correct major key, it stays in the minor, increasing the music's feeling of soulful pathos with every bar.

The tune is so beautiful, and its continuation so expressive, that you feel it could go on like this forever, and indeed the only way for Mozart to get the clarinetist under control is to do some-thing drastic. And so at 8:26, the music runs into a dissonant chord, the musical equivalent of snapping your fingers under the nose of a daydreamer to bring him or her back to earth. In a flash, the music continues in the proper major key as if noth-ing at all had happened. The reverie is over, and Mozart has just demonstrated that pathos and wit can coexist simultaneously, while beautifully illustrating that the necessary reestablishment of the home key that so satisfyingly rounds off a sonata movement demands that the themes continue to evolve and change over the course of the recapitulation.

At 8:30 the cadence theme returns, now greatly expanded with additional material. Indeed, it almost seems as if the motion music of the development is about to break in once again, but the clarinet dismisses the notion with a descending chromatic scale (at 9:14). A final trill on clarinet, second violin, and viola leads to the wittily foreshortened version of the opening question/answer, and the movement ends with exactly the same gesture as did the exposition. The point of this last musical digression and the preceding one (the recapitulation of the second subject in the clarinet) is that both require an obvious "correction" that emphasizes the home key, and this in turn provides that feeling of formal closure the music needs.

From these last events, we also discover an important fact about sonata form movements in general, which is that the best way to convince us that we are in the home key is not to simply stay there uneventfully for minutes at a time but rather to show signs of leaving it only to continually and emphatically return. This practice has the dual function of sustaining the music's harmonic tension right up to the end while making it extra clear exactly where we are all the while. It also gives Mozart the opportunity to save his most telling surprises for the closing moments—like any good storyteller—and so justifies the time he takes getting there.

I hope that having listened to the entire movement, noticing these characteristically Mozartean elements along the way, you will be impressed not just by the music's gentle beauty but also by its simplicity and directness. Descriptions of form unfortunately risk making music sound mechanical, as though the composer finds himself shackled to a process that controls him, rather than the reality, which is just the opposite. In the closing pages of the first movement of his Clarinet Quartet, what Mozart is basically saying to his listeners is this: "I have a gorgeous tune, and I know how to make it even more gorgeous when it comes back. At the same time, I need to create a climax and end the movement in the most satisfying possible way. And I want to do both, because I'm not going to sacrifice one for the other." Finding musically captivating, expressive solutions to problems like these is the stuff of great art, and no one was better at it than Mozart.

Part 2

Chamber Music

Introduction

As seen at the end of "Musical Form in the Classical Period," in considering the epic Divertimento for string trio, K. 563, the only thing small about chamber music is the number of players involved. Mozart's chamber music routinely exceeds his orchestral music in length and scale. When you think about it a little, this really isn't surprising. Music written to be played at home, at a gathering of friends, or for a small group of connoisseurs can afford to take its time and to indulge in ambitious formal designs that would confound a large group of orchestral musicians. What chamber music lacks in sheer color and dynamic range, it more than makes up for in rhythmic subtlety, harmonic richness, and intimacy of expression.

Haydn, Mozart, and their contemporaries created the forms and styles of chamber music that still thrive today, and they did it by writing works in which each voice is independent but also part of the larger ensemble. Prior to them, if you listen to any piece of instrumental music from the baroque period (roughly 1600–1750), you will hear an extra keyboard or plucked string instrument (harpsichord, organ, lute, harp, and so forth) playing along with the ensemble and supplying a bass line and harmonic accompaniment in chords, just as a guitar or piano may accompany a singer. For baroque composers, instruments, like voices, always needed some sort of support, and by relegating this support to a special instrument or group of instruments (called the *continuo*), they were free to focus on the solo instrumental or vocal lines above.

The result of this conception is that in the baroque period, a designation such as "trio" does not tell you how many players the piece requires, but rather the number of distinct musical "parts" or voices that it's written for. A typical *trio sonata,* for example, the most popular chamber music genre of Bach's day, if written for strings and continuo can include as many as four or even five players, depending on which instruments the performers choose to use in realizing the bass line and supporting harmony. On the other hand, works such as Bach's organ trios require only a single player, the three parts being covered by the organist's two hands on the upper parts and his or her feet on the lower one.

In classical-period chamber music, however, each ensemble is self-sufficient, creating its own harmony, melody, and accompaniment, with each voice having to function both as soloist and support. What you see, numerically, is exactly what you get. The medium that expressed this new independence best is the string quartet as perfected by Haydn. The reason that four players became the norm is very logical: you need three notes to form basic chords in any key, and thus to provide a full harmonic support for a melody. Add another performer who gets the tune and the magic number is four, while having them all come from the same family of instruments ensures a smooth blend of timbres. This doesn't mean that chamber groups of fewer players can't exist; certainly they do, particularly if one of the participants is a pianist, the piano having the ability to make a complete mass of harmony all by itself.

So in general, chamber music in the classical period falls into three broad categories: music for homogeneous ensembles of melody instruments, usually strings; music for mixed ensembles consisting of melody instruments (strings, winds, brass) and instruments that can also provide a full harmonic accompaniment alone, such as a piano; music for mixed groups of melody instruments (such as Mozart's Clarinet Quintet and the wind serenades). Each type presents its own special challenges, because the one unalterable rule in all classical chamber music, especially as practiced by Mozart, is that every single part must be necessary and no single part should dominate to the extent that the others are permanently reduced to mere accompaniment.

The sonata style, with its natural tendency to treat melodies as characters in a dramatic narrative, made this new way of writing instrumental music possible—or perhaps, in order to avoid the "chicken and the egg" argument about what came first, it's better to say that the form and the method arose more or less simultaneously and were mutually influential. However historians choose to view the matter, the fact remains that no one wrote more sonata-form movements in chamber music than did Mozart. This is what allowed him to expand the scale of his music to such an unprecedented degree, but the point to keep in mind is that the increase in size is fully justified by the increase in the expressive richness of the melodic content, as you will hear for yourself.

The Piano Quartets

Piano Quartet in G Minor, K. 478 (1785)
Piano Quartet in E-flat Major, K. 493 (1786)

With these two great works, Mozart basically invented this genre, later taken up with great success by Schumann, Brahms, and Dvořák. A piano quartet requires, in addition to the keyboard soloist, the ensemble best known as a *string trio*—a violin, a viola, and a cello. It makes sense to discuss these two pieces together, because they have many formal similarities and the compositional challenge in creating them was the same (and they also tend to come coupled together on recordings). Each has three movements, arranged in fast–slow–fast pattern. All six movements are in sonata form, but it would be a real mistake to say that the form of each movement is the same. For example, Mozart calls the finale of the G Minor Piano Quartet a rondo, and although he doesn't say so, the finale of K. 493 is one too, but a very special, hybrid kind that combines features of sonata form with those of the rondo. This isn't nearly as complicated as it sounds, and it pays big musical dividends as you will see shortly.

Because the piano can make a complete mass of harmony all by itself, sounding as many notes simultaneously as the performer has fingers, there is a natural tendency for the three string players to unite in opposition, to take individual leading roles as soloists accompanied by the piano or by the remaining strings, or any combination of these. The result offers many opportunities for variations in tone color and texture, and Mozart takes full advantage of this fact. In general, however, the Quartet in E-flat keeps the string trio together in opposition to the piano more consistently than does the work in G minor. This gives the major-key work a bigger, more massive quality when compared to the wiry compactness of its predecessor. The difference is most clearly audible in the outer movements of each work.

For example, the G Minor Quartet begins with a stern question-and-answer opening theme in abrupt phrases containing the "Mozart rhythm" (dum, dum, dadum). The E-flat Quartet, in contrast, opens with broad chords for the full ensemble. The contrast extends to the second subjects: that of the G Minor Quartet is one of Mozart's nursery-rhyme themes in short phrases, and its innocent sweetness sounds oddly disturbing when it appears in its minor-key version in the recapitulation. The second subject of K. 493, on the other hand, is a long-limbed melody, for solo violin accompanied by the piano and, later, the remaining strings.

The first-movement development sections confirm the very different characters of the two works. That of K. 478 is very short and episodic (that is, based mostly on new material). It seems hardly to have gotten started when the strings interrupt repeatedly with the opening question and so initiate the recapitulation. The development section of the E-flat Quartet, by contrast, is huge, and obsessively based entirely on a tiny, five-note motive (with a little decorative "turn" in the middle) that comes from the transition theme that leads to the second subject. Starting out with many repetitions of this short idea, Mozart gradually lengthens and broadens the phrasing until the music majestically alights at the recapitulation like a large jet making a particularly smooth landing. As I hope you will take the time to hear for yourself, you don't have to be especially conscious of the form to enjoy any of these points, which are plainly audible as simple contrasts of melody and texture.

Sonata-form slow movements present few if any problems for listeners. Whenever you encounter one, you need worry about nothing except the beauty of the tunes. Musically speaking, however, "slow" always means "long," since so much time gets used in the simple business of playing the main themes. Quite a few slow movements in sonata form, such as that of the G Minor Piano Quartet, will simply leave out the development section altogether and have the basic form ABAB (although here each subject includes whole groups of themes and motives). If, as in the Piano Quartet in E-flat, however, the form is more orthodox (with the standard repeats and a real development section), then the movement is going to sound very much like a glorified ABA, only with the whole exposition section comprising A, and B consisting of the development (which often introduces entirely new material for contrast). Either way the form merely enhances and directs the music's ongoing lyrical flow. Just wallow in it.

As I mentioned above, the two finales combine the scale of sonata form with the more relaxed, episodic character of a rondo, which has the basic form ABACA. Start with a standard sonata-form exposition, and make the opening melody, or first subject, the ritornello theme of your rondo. This gives you section A. The second subject in the new key then becomes section B, or the first episode. Repeat A before moving on to the next episode, or section C, actually a big development section based either on earlier material or entirely new themes (or both). Finally, recapitulate your two subjects in reverse order: BA, so that the final appearance of A provides a satisfying conclusion to the movement, as in most rondos (recall the discussion of form in "Musical Form in the Classical Period," and in particular the idea of ending a movement with the melody of its opening). This gives us ABACBA, or the "sonata-rondo" as Mozart uses it here. This clever method enjoys the singular advantage of offering the sense of formal relaxation typical of the rondo form with the sheer scale of a sonata movement, and so allows Mozart to create two finales that perfectly balance the weight of each work's opening.

Having noted these similarities, you will also notice that these two finales further affirm the basic contrast between the two works. Although the finale of the G Minor Quartet turns to the major key (and an opening tune that strikingly appears in several other of Mozart's works only slightly varied, most notably as the second subject of Piano Concerto No. 23's first movement), it also has a second subject of nursery-rhyme character in the Mozartean shape of two halves that are mirror images of each other (two phrases of seven notes, the first descending and the second ascending). Tactics such as this constitute an important way of unifying a large work. Unlike a typical habit of the romantic period, composers of Mozart's day seldom recall themes from earlier movements in later ones, preferring the contrast of new material whenever possible. But they will often repeat music of a certain style or character, and to this extent, one has to understand that an "idea" is not just a specific tune or rhythm, but also a certain type of texture, mood, or tone color.

In the finale of the E-flat Quartet, the opposition between string trio and piano has become so polarized that the strings have very few passages at all when they do not play as a complete unit. So once again Mozart achieves unity over the course of the work by adopting a strategy, in this case consistent treatment of texture, which frees him to fill up his finale with fresh new themes. The essential point in considering these two pieces (which strike me as the perfect introduction to Mozart's chamber works in general) is to realize that the challenge he so triumphantly meets is the need to offer the maximum amount of variety (both formal and melodic) given the natural limitations of the medium. It's a fact that looms even larger in the next work under consideration.

Piano and Wind Quintet in E-flat Major, K. 452 (1784)

This magnificent piece inspired Beethoven to write his own work for similar forces, and the two almost always come coupled together on recordings. At the time that he completed the quintet in 1784, Mozart wrote to his father that he thought it the best thing he had written up to that time. Not all composers are the best judges of their own work, but Mozart had no illusions in this respect.

I discussed in my initial presentation of the piano quartets how in a situation where one participant (the pianist) is musically self-sufficient, there's a tendency to pit the keyboard instrument against the three strings together. Here there are four winds: oboe, clarinet, horn, and bassoon, and while a similar solution suggests itself in terms of the interaction between piano and winds, Mozart faces the additional challenge of creating a harmonious blend from four instruments of very different tone color. In addition, the winds can't sustain a long melody for bars at a time without taking a breath, and so need to pause more frequently.

In the first movement, Mozart solves this problem in two ways. First, he begins with a slow introduction full of majestic march figures alternating with long, flowing wind solos accompanied by rippling piano figurations. This creates the impression of "bigness" of design while also allowing him to suggest those broadly lyrical lines he so loves, even though at this slow tempo those flights of song are really only a couple of bars long and aren't at all difficult to play. The allegro, in sonata form, exploits the possibilities of dialogue to the full. Both the first and second subjects consist of question-and-answer-type melodies played twice, with piano and winds exchanging parts each time. The second subject's answer is particularly delicious, a dizzy phrase brimming with wit.

The development section is tiny, but potent. It hardly develops anything. It consists of a series of short phrases from the first subject posed by individual wind players, like musical question marks, so when the recapitulation chimes in with its regular phrases, it once again sounds "bigger" and more regular than it really is. Mozart enhances this impression by returning briefly to the mood of the development after the first subject—a threat of going backwards. But this is just a feint, because by jettisoning the exposition's transition themes and cutting straight to the second subject, Mozart in fact achieves amazing formal conciseness while all the while creating the illusion of leisure and expansiveness.

The gorgeous slow movement, marked *larghetto* (a little slow), is also in full sonata form. Here Mozart returns to the technique of the first movement's introduction, and once again note that he creates unity by recalling musical styles and gestures rather than actual melodies. The opening is a graceful dialogue between the piano and winds, while the transition to the second subject features more of those stunning, long lines from clarinet, oboe, horn, and bassoon (in that order) over rippling piano figurations, leading to an athematic passage of pure wind harmony with still more gentle piano accompaniment. When the second subject arrives, the winds accompany the piano in a surprising reversal of roles, and when the left hand of the piano takes over the repeated chords of this accompaniment, the right hand underlines the broad wind phrases with shorter interjections.

Mozart achieves bigness of design in this movement, which is actually very modest in length (only about seven minutes including repeats), by giving listeners a development section based on entirely new material. This maximizes the contrast with the return of the first subject, particularly as the development ends with another passage of softly sustained, cloudy harmony in the winds. Mozart greatly extends the flowing transitional passage the second time around and introduces the second subject with a thrilling rising chromatic scale for the full ensemble that creates almost unbearable tension. So despite the slow tempo of the music, it's anything but uneventful, and like the first movement, it never sounds short-winded (pardon the pun)—quite the opposite in fact.

The finale is a sonata-rondo of the type just encountered in the piano quartets. Once again the movement is actually comparatively short (about six minutes), and once again it sounds bigger than it is. As in the piano quartets, Mozart achieves the "rondo" by returning to his opening theme (the first subject) before the development section, and then recapitulates the second subject prior to rounding off the movement with the return of the first subject. But before that happy event, the music stops dead in its tracks and the five players entertain listeners with a cadenza— normally a passage of free improvisation, but in this case it isn't improvised at all. Mozart writes the whole thing out, and it only *sounds* improvised. Once again this tactic enlarges the listener's subjective impression of this otherwise very pithy form, simply through delaying the return of the opening theme by interposing some new material in an obviously free style (compare the similar impact of the slow movement's development section). After the return of the first subject, the piece ends with a delicious coda full of lightness and conspiratorial wit.

Six String Quartets
Dedicated to Haydn

String Quartet No. 14 in G Major, K. 387 (1782)
String Quartet No. 15 in D Minor, K. 421 (1783)
String Quartet No. 16 in E-flat Major, K. 428 (1783)
String Quartet No. 17 in B-flat Major, K. 458 (1784)
String Quartet No. 18 in A Major, K. 464 (1785)
String Quartet No. 19 in C Major, K. 465 (1785)

The literature on these particular quartets is vast, but nothing summarizes their special character better than Mozart's original dedication to Haydn and the older man's comments to Mozart's father Leopold on hearing the actual music.

Mozart's dedication:

> To my dear friend Haydn:
>
> Having decided to send his children out into the wide world, a father resolves to entrust them to the care and protection of a famous man of his age, who is luckily also his best friend. Here then, celebrated man and my dearest friend, are my six sons. They truly are the fruit of a long and diligent effort. Still, the hope to see this effort (which was supported by many friends) at least partially rewarded has encouraged me; and I will be happy if these pieces will one day be a consolation to me. You yourself, dearest friend, during your last visit to this capital, signaled to me your satisfaction. Your opinion, above all, inspires me to recommend them to you, and makes me hope that you will not consider them unworthy of your high regard. Please accept them cordially, and be their father, guide and

friend! From this moment I cede to you my rights to them, and I beg that you look with indulgence on their defects—which the biased eye of a father might have missed—and continue nevertheless to give them your priceless friendship while I remain with all my heart,

Your Sincerest Friend, W.A.M.
Vienna, September 1, 1785

Haydn's remark to Leopold Mozart:

Before God and as an honest man, I tell you that your son is the greatest composer known to me in person or by reputation. He has taste and what is more, the most profound knowledge of composition.

Haydn wasn't kidding, and neither was Mozart. He lavished three years of effort on these pieces, composed neither on commission nor for his immediately personal use, but as a true act of homage to the man whose String Quartets Op. 33 showed Mozart what classical chamber music could be. Partisans of each composer have long squabbled over exactly what Haydn's influence of Mozart was and how much it really mattered, but the simple fact is that before Mozart's encounter with these Haydn string quartets, there isn't a single one of his early works in the genre that has retained a secure place in the active repertoire today.

Here's a simple table that provides an overview of the formal design of the six "Haydn" Quartets, which will serve as useful points of reference in discussing the individual works.

Six Quartets Dedicated to Haydn

Movement	K. 387	K. 421	K. 428	K.458	K.464	K. 465
1	Sonata	Sonata	Sonata	Sonata	Sonata	Sonata
2	Minuet	ABA	Sonata	Minuet	Minuet	Sonata*
3	Sonata*	Minuet	Minuet	Sonata*	Variations	Minuet
4	Sonata	Variations	Rondo	Sonata	Sonata	Sonata

* without development section

As you can see, Mozart adopts a wide range of forms and varies the order of his inner movements so that half of the time the minuet comes second, rather than third as is almost the invariable rule in the symphonies. But the element most characteristic of these six pieces, and the most important lesson that Mozart acquired from Haydn, is that special conversational quality so important to establishing the equality of the four voices and engaging the listener's attention with the characterful interplay of melodic lines. This did not come easily to Mozart.

I have already discussed the basis of Mozart's style in vocal music, in the act of singing and the creation of beautiful, long-limbed melodies simply accompanied. The difference between this style, instrumentally speaking, and that of the string quartet can be compared to the difference between singing and speaking. Creating the musical equivalent of an ongoing conversation (at least in fast movements) requires short motives tossed from one player to the next, and a regular recourse to contrapuntal textures to represent the more involved musical "discussions." Absorbing these elements into his naturally expansive view of form and reconciling them with his love of vocal melody took much time and work, but as Haydn himself acknowledged, Mozart achieved his aims with complete success.

This matters to listeners, because along with this conversational quality comes the possibility of expressing not just the usual happiness or cheer, but wit. In short, Haydn gave Mozart's music a sense of humor, and this had an incalculable impact not just on his instrumental works but also on the great comic operas to come. It's surely no coincidence that the first of these, *The Abduction from the Seraglio,* K. 384, dates from the same year (1782) as the G Major Quartet, K 387.

The expression of humor was Haydn's great achievement in his own six Op. 33 quartets. In these works the traditional minuet is replaced with a scherzo, which means "joke," and one of the quartets is actually called "The Joke" (it is indeed very funny). Mozart tends not to poke fun the way Haydn does, but between the two of them, each in his own style, real humor—as distinct from superficial cheer—entered the language of music. It's often said that Mozart's mature symphonies and chamber works speak the language of comic opera, and so they do, but both the operas and the instrumental pieces would have been much less comic had it not been for the lessons learned and sublimated in these quartets.

String Quartet No. 14 in G Major, K. 387

Right from the very start, you will notice this music's conversation quality (and I'll take that as a given in considering the remaining pieces in the set). The opening isn't so much a tune as it is a discussion among the four players. A brief transition featuring rising chromatic scales (that is, moving upward by successive half steps) introduces a highly contrasted second subject as simple in harmony and phrasing as a college fight-song. The extreme brevity of the exposition makes this one of Mozart's most concise movements, but he more than makes up for it in the minuet, which is one of the longest ever written (about eight minutes in most performances) and full of Haydnesque rhythmic games as well as more Mozartean rising chromatic scales in connection with them.

The slow movement provides yet another example of sonata form without development. As noted previously, in many of these cases a full development section would make the movement very long and distract attention from the main focus, which is the lyrical beauty of the melodies themselves. Also, just as much of the way that sonata-movement themes develop arises from the restatement of the transitional material and second subject in the recapitulation, in all of these instances Mozart takes the opportunity to expand and decorate his melodies accordingly on their return. They do indeed develop, but in keeping with the classical ideal, only as much as they need to in order to enhance their expressiveness and no more.

The finale contrasts contrapuntal writing with simply accompanied melody, all at high speed. I said in the first chapter that you won't encounter many fugues in Mozart, but you will run into *fugatos,* which are fugal expositions of themes that then give way to some other kind of material. Both the first and second subjects are fugatos, in which the same material is stated at staggered intervals by each instrument, and the second subject actually tosses in the first as well for good measure. Notice that the development reintroduces those slithery rising chromatic scales from the first movement and minuet, one of those effective little touches that enhances the listener's subconscious sense of the work's fundamental unity of inspiration.

String Quartet No. 15 in D Minor, K. 421

This is the only quartet in the set in a minor key and the only one with a theme-and-variations finale, and these special features give it a very singular character. The opening tune gives off an extraordinary feeling of deep sadness, but perhaps the most remarkable thing about the exposition is that is represents a gradual transition from darkness to light, which Mozart accomplishes both harmonically and rhythmically. The second subject is in a bright major key, but even more significantly, its accompaniment has sixteen notes to the bar as opposed to the opening's eight, so that although the tempo is the same, the music seems to double in speed. The positively ethereal cadence theme that brings the exposition to a close is faster still, twenty-four notes per measure, and played in the upper registers of the instruments that have the melody.

The structure of this exposition leads to dire consequences in the recapitulation, which Mozart characteristically rewrites so as to remain in the tonic minor key. This means that the effect of "brightening" becomes instead a mood of increasing agitation and despair as the underlying rhythms accelerate, and Mozart does everything he can melodically as well in recomposing his second subject to enhance its "minorness." Mozart seldom writes whole works around minor keys, but when he does, he never holds back, and the sheer intensity of his "minor-key manner" has earned these pieces universal admiration from scholars and music lovers alike.

Such emotional density in the first movement calls forth a con- soling, hymnlike slow movement in simple ABA form. In most performances, the initial statement of A, which is in two halves, will observe Mozart's indicated repeats with the great benefit of telling you where exactly where B starts, although there are two passionate outbursts framing this section that also serve to make the melodic organization of the movement especially clear. This formal simplicity is also characteristic of the refreshingly direct minuet, with the second violin and viola following the sharp rhythms of first violin and cello in lock step for bars at a time. The trio is a charming German dance for solo violin with *pizzicato* (plucked) accompaniment.

There's something half-sinister, half-humorous about the fina- le's variation subject. With its galloping rhythm and a repeated note refrain at the end of each phrase, it brings to mind such oddities as Tom Lehrer's *Irish Ballad,* and the four ensuing varia- tions (a fifth, consisting of the tune played once through at high speed without repeats, provides the coda) do nothing to dispel the emotional ambiguity that hangs over the music. This was also one of Mozart's special gifts: the understanding that sometimes issues in life don't resolve cleanly in favor of happiness or sadness, but rather hover somewhere in between. Many later composers picked up on this idea, but few expressed it as economically and directly as Mozart does here.

String Quartet No. 16 in E-flat Major, K. 428

The opening of this quartet describes vividly the destabilizing power of chromatic harmony. It begins with a strange-sounding unison phrase for all four strings, whose chromaticism defines no definite key at all. Neither does the melodic sequel, and it's only several seconds later, at the arrival of the first loud chord, that Mozart favors listeners with clear, unambiguous harmony, and in doing so repeats the opening phrase on this new foundation, as if to say: "We were in the home key all along, only you just didn't notice it." The whole opening is, in fact, yet another example of Mozartean wit in action. This sort of harmonic cat-and-mouse game gives the movement a somewhat poker-faced quality, necessary if the joke is to work each time that same music returns. You can always be sure that when Mozart takes the trouble to begin a movement more or less in suspense, he will do everything he can to enhance that initial impression later on.

The same contrast characterizes the slow second movement, which is in regular sonata form with a tiny development section based on the second half of the first subject, all supported by a flowing accompaniment that hardly ever stops. But when it does, remarkable things happen, particularly in the transition between the first and second subjects. This contains some truly weird, dissonant harmony, which gets even weirder in the recapitulation. The slow tempo only enhances the alarming impact of Mozart's pungent excursion to distant tonal territory, and the entire passage is about as "far out" as he gets.

Harmonic ambiguity goes hand in hand with emotional ambiguity, and Mozart balances the "intellectual" or abstract first half of the work with one of his wittiest and most cheerful second halves. The minuet might have come straight from Haydn, with its sturdy rhythms and rustic hurdy-gurdy imitations, while the finale is a riot, thanks to a delicious main theme that seems to wink at the listener gleefully as it whizzes by. Haydn was a master at creating this sort of tune, but Mozart has learned his lesson well, not least in contriving the most amusing lead-ins each time it returns. What began in mystery, then, ultimately ends in a blaze of high spirits.

String Quartet No. 17 in B-flat Major, K. 458 ("The Hunt")

The nickname of this quartet, "The Hunt," comes from the propulsive first movement, which is in the galloping, "hunting" rhythm of 6/8. Its tunes, based on simple chords and openly spaced harmonies, have an outdoors quality, with the strings called upon to imitate the sound of French horns. This is, in fact, one of the few instrumental works by Mozart that actually describes some form of activity other than the dance, and there will be more to come in the next quartet. Hunting music of this type was very popular with the eighteenth-century aristocracy, and Haydn's music is full of it. The entire work deliberately maintains an aristocratic poise throughout its four movements.

For example, the moderately paced minuet (placed second) stands among Mozart's most graciously courtly—indeed, it's far more so that the large quantity of real dance music that the Austrian emperor actually paid him to produce. The slow movement, another sample of sonata form without repeats or a development section, revels in the sort of highly ornamented melody characteristic of the baroque period. Mozart's attention to detail here is simply exquisite. Even the vivacious finale finds room for a gently flowing second subject that contrasts strongly with the populist character of its surroundings. This is, in sum, aristocratic music for the nobility as they wished to see themselves, and as much as Mozart was a rebellious free spirit, he was also an employee of more than one court. No one knew better than he how to idealize their more virtuous qualities in music.

String Quartet No. 18 in A Major, K. 464

A work unashamedly designed more for connoisseurs than for casual listeners, this quartet offers genuine riches that reward as much attention as you have to spare. It's an ostentatiously intellectual work, and perhaps for that reason it has never enjoyed quite as much acclaim as its comrades—particularly "The Hunt" and the Quartet in D Minor. Much of its thematic material has a deliberately neutral flavor, not because it's in any way inexpressive or because Mozart was having a bad day, but because he wants to focus listeners' attention on the grand structure he builds out of the simplest materials and the expressive transformations to which he subjects them.

Take the very opening: two descending phrases, followed by two little melodic turns. Nothing could be simpler, and the entire movement is built out of these elements. It is, in fact, an example (as is the finale) of a favorite practice of Haydn's: *monothematic* sonata form. This simply means that the same basic material, not necessarily literally repeated but close enough in derivation, does duty for both first and second subjects. The fascination in such a technique lies in the exceptional feeling of unity it creates, and as you can well imagine, monothematic sonata movements tend to be quite compact.

This particular example lasts about seven and a half minutes on average, including the exposition repeat. There's actually quite a bit of contrast, but it occurs less between the two subjects than between them and the transitional material. The development section treats each clause of the opening gesture extensively, with the descending phrase becoming very chromatic and acquiring the character of a gentle sigh that rapidly becomes a wailing storm of falling musical lines. When the recapitulation finally arrives, it comes as a positive relief and proves yet again that in Mozart there is no conflict between formal virtuosity and expressive intensity.

To make matters even more difficult for himself, Mozart puts the first movement in the same meter (3/4) and basic tempo as the ensuing minuet, and yet the two pieces don't sound at all alike because the themes themselves are so different, with the first movement's phrases gliding over the bar lines and the minuet operating largely within them in shorter, more rhythmic fragments. If the first half of the work takes place entirely in triple rhythm, the remainder is in *duple rhythm* (in "two"), a dichotomy that neatly divides the work into rhythmic opposites.

The third movement's variations are both relatively short (because the theme itself is short) and easy to follow. The first four of them are regular (that is, they fall into two halves, both repeated), with the fourth marking a clear change to a somber minor key. Mozart varies the repeats in the gently elegiac, major-key fifth variation, and remarkably accompanies the sixth with a drum rhythm on the cello that persists all the way through without pause. This may not exactly be Ravel's *Boléro*, but it's a curiously disturbing effect, and one as evocative as the horn imitations in "The Hunt's" first movement. As the sixth variation draws to a close, the persistent rhythm rises through the other three parts, leading at last to a return of the opening theme, but it's the drum rhythm in the cello that has the final say. As in the first movement, what started out sounding somewhat plain evolves into something expressively remarkable.

As mentioned, the finale is also in monothematic sonata form, and in duple meter like the third movement, but that's not the most wonderful thing about it. What Mozart achieves here is both a simplification and intensification of the first movement's opening. The descending phrase gets reduced to a falling chromatic fragment of four notes, not repeated as in the first movement, but followed immediately by the first movement's second phrase, the little melodic turn. Here you can see one of the most powerful examples of the mosaic type of construction (building a large structure out of tiny motives) mentioned in "What Makes Mozart Sound Like Mozart." At the same time, Mozart creates large-scale unity over the length of the whole quartet.

The unstable tonality and familiar shape of the themes makes this finale an effective continuation of the first movement's development section, with the interesting result that the simpler phrasing and rhythmic treatment typical of a finale actually produces an emotional intensification. This so undercuts the music's ostensibly major-key demeanor that the quartet ends in a whisper, the players seeming to say: "Yes, it's A major, but please don't tell anyone!" Pieces that end quietly almost never enjoy the popularity of "grand finale" style works, even in chamber music, but you can't listen to these ambivalent last few bars without feeling that Mozart's ending is not only the right one but the only possible one. This quartet is a musical tour-de-force, and perhaps Mozart's most comprehensive tribute to Haydn in its treatment of form.

String Quartet No. 19 in C Major, K. 465 ("Dissonance")

The incredibly creepy slow introduction exposes listeners once again to the world of chromatic harmony. Mozart begins with a harmonically bizarre introduction, for no purpose other than to shock. It certainly works. When the allegro finally arrives (and the introduction isn't a note too long), it proves to be as expansive as that of the previous quartet was terse. The big exposition contains numerous melodic figures, racy transitions, and a big, fat second subject, all sounding even freer and easier than usual because of that strange opening. Here the movement's quiet ending means exactly the opposite of the similar gesture that concluded the A Major Quartet: it's Mozart's witty way of telling listeners that the introduction was no big deal after all, while the healthy, bustling minuet that follows only confirms this impression. The slow movement, the last example of sonata form without repeats or development, has a harmonically arresting second subject that builds itself up one part at a time over a grinding cello rhythm—strikingly recalling the A Major Quartet's "drum music" variation—and it's that disturbing rhythm that has the last word.

Mozart has one more surprise in store in the finale: a wonderfully warm excursion in its second subject to a distant key. Listen for a passage of rapid fiddling from the first violin, and then, just over a minute into the movement, you'll hear the most remarkable effect—somewhat like looking through a lens and refocusing on a distant object so that it becomes momentarily clear while leaving the foreground blurry, only to reverse the process a few seconds later. In the recapitulation, the need to rewrite the second subject to keep it in the tonic key gives Mozart the opportunity to double your pleasure.

Mozart composed four more string quartets (K. 490, K. 575, K. 589, and K. 590) in the six years remaining to him after the completion of this set. By general consent, however, he never surpassed in this medium the variety, craftsmanship, emotional depth, and wit that characterizes these pieces, composed as a true labor of love and dedicated by one of the two greatest composers of his era to the other, who was also his best friend.

The String Quintets

String Quintet in C Minor, K. 406 (1788)
String Quintet in C Major, K. 515 (1787)
String Quintet in G Minor, K. 516 (1787)*
String Quintet in D Major, K. 593 (1790)
String Quintet in E-flat Major, K. 614 (1791)

In considering what many view as Mozart's greatest chamber works, one first needs to address a couple of housekeeping matters. There is an additional early Quintet in B-flat Major, K. 174, which I am not going to discuss here, although it's a charming work, and if you purchase a set of the quintets, it may well be included. The reason that Mozart composed these works is not fully known, although absent any evidence to the contrary (as we have in the case of the "Haydn" Quartets), one can be reasonably sure that they were written "on spec" in order to try to secure a court appointment, at least as regards the two works of 1787.

There is good reason to make this assumption, because Mozart eventually decided to have them published by subscription, which means no one paid to secure the exclusive rights to them (as would have been the case with a formal commission), and we know he did not receive any specific aristocratic recognition related to them. Because such publications required at least three works (and more commonly six), Mozart added the Quintet in C Minor, K. 406, which is actually a transcription of the Wind Serenade No. 12, K. 388 (in the same key). It's always

---

* See also "What Makes Mozart Sound Like Mozart?"

fun to listen to transcriptions, particularly when they are done by the original composer, so I have included the quintet in the above list, even though I will not discuss it until we come to consider the chamber music for wind ensemble, where it more properly belongs.

The evening the String Quintet in G Minor was played in the home of one of Mozart's friends, with Mozart and Haydn taking the two viola parts, must have been some performance! The reason these works aren't better known has nothing to with their artistic value, which is universally acknowledged, but with economics. There are no standing ensembles dedicated to the string quintet repertoire, largely because it's so tiny when it comes to generally acknowledged "great works." Mozart (6), Brahms (2), Beethoven (1), Schubert (1), and Dvořák (3) account for the most important examples, and the total number that they wrote, as you can see, amounts to only thirteen. From this an ensemble can't exactly make a career, even though there are dozens of fine works by lesser well-known composers that would well repay some attention.

Quintets, then, are generally played by quartets, plus an additional player hired for the occasion. The practicality of this approach becomes even more evident upon considering that, unlike the string quartet, there's no hard-and-fast rule as to the exact composition of a string quintet. Mozart's contemporary, Luigi Boccherini, pioneered the genre for two violins, viola, and two cellos. Schubert follows Boccherini. Mozart prefers two violas instead of two cellos, as do Brahms and Dvořák (in two out of his three cases—one work asks for normal string quartet plus double bass).

There is something about the string quintet that ideally fits Mozart's style. He himself offers the best clue to its special character when he says in his dedication to Haydn that the quartets were the "fruit of a long and diligent effort." Fine as they are,

Mozart's quartets make a point of being "effortful." They are intellectually powerful, diverse works crafted with immense discipline as a tribute from one musician to another, engaging the mind as much as the heart. The quintets, on the other hand, operate at a more primal expressive level. Though no less superb in their formal virtuosity, they are more melodically luxurious and emotionally extravagant—like a sinfully rich dessert that's never too heavy or cloying, but leaves you always wanting more.

Leaving aside analogous comparisons, the difference between Mozart's quartets and quintets can be quantified very simply in terms that already have been discussed: the contrast between musical conversation and song. In his six "Haydn" Quartets, Mozart mastered the art of the conversation and greatly enriched his stylistic range in the process. But his first love, his natural element, involved turning his instruments loose and letting them sing, and having five players instead of four adds just enough extra color, textural variety, weight of tone, and possibilities for dramatic contrast to give Mozart the opportunity to let his ensemble rhapsodize in song that much more often. That doesn't make the quintets necessarily *better*—just different. Mozart really never misses the chance to utilize to the fullest every resource available—in this case, a single extra viola player—as a means of giving each medium, and each work within that medium, as much individual character as possible.

String Quintet in C Major, K. 515 (1787)

This first movement is huge, almost a quarter of an hour long (with exposition repeat), and Mozart makes it huge in the simplest possible way: by writing a really expansive exposition with lots of themes and internal repetition. The first subject is a series of question-and-answer motives against a rapid repeated-note accompaniment, immediately echoed in the tonic minor. Despite attempts to move elsewhere, the music stubbornly returns to this incredibly distinctive texture before moving on to the second subject. In "What Makes Mozart Sound Like Mozart," I discussed how one of the best ways in sonata form to establish a key while maintaining the necessary energy level of a quick movement is actually to seem to leave it, only to keep returning. The result here creates a feeling of spaciousness with no loss of energy.

The second subject also offers a range of material, including a cadence theme featuring a musical "squiggle" that sounds a bit like a slowed-down version of the opening of the *Marriage of Figaro* overture. Because the exposition is so long and varied, Mozart makes the development quite short and simple. It features the opening gesture (one hesitates to call it a "theme"), followed by a plenitude of expanded squiggles atop which bits of the second subject come and go. That's really all there is to it. It leads triumphantly back to the first subject, obviously relieved not to have to keep developing, and Mozart colorfully recapitulates all the original material, letting the movement wind down to a wittily quiet ending. All this massive simplicity stands in stark contrast to Mozart's more deliberately sophisticated quartet style.

Placed second, the minuet and trio share the same tempo, so there's no clear division between them other than the different themes each section uses. Unusually, the trio is much the longer part, and it features some typically Mozartean creepy chromatic harmony to give listeners a jolt or two. The slow movement employs Mozart's favorite "sonata form without development," but this is deceptive, because what listeners actually hear are two duets between first violin and first viola—one serene and a touch coy, the other more urgently passionate—separated by interludes. The finale has the same form as the slow movement, but the effect is essentially that of a rondo because of the repetitions of its winsome main theme, which Mozart also brings back at the very end to round off the form just as rondos do typically.

The big development of the finale's first subject that Mozart inserts into his recapitulation also has the feel of a distinct episode, and so, contrary to what you may imagine by my use of the word *development,* this actually loosens the form by making it seem more sectional. You may also notice that the second subject contains a prominent sudden excursion to a distant key very similar to that in the finale of the "Dissonance" Quartet, which interestingly is also in the home key of C major. But note that in the quartet Mozart deepens and expands this passage quite thrillingly when it returns, whereas in the quintet he merely repeats it and moves on.

String Quintet in G Minor, K. 516 (1787)

For most of its first three movements and a good bit of its fourth, the G Minor Quintet stands as one of the saddest pieces of music ever. Much biographical ink has been spilled over what in Mozart's life could possibly have inspired such intensity of feeling, as though a musician needs an external cause in order to explore the expressive bounds of his art, and the only "deep" or "intense" emotions are necessarily miserable ones. The C Major Quintet is, in fact, one of Mozart's most profoundly happy and contented works. When you note that this "evil twin" was composed at the same time, and further take into account Mozart's veritable obsession with pushing every medium in which he worked to its formal and expressive limits (within the boundaries of classical style), then the need to find the "story behind the work" vanishes like the puff of smoke theories such as these inevitably resemble on closer examination.

The evidence for spontaneous musical generation becomes even stronger if one compares Mozart's practice in the first movements of both works. Certainly the tonalities involved are different, as are the themes, but consider also the similarities. The most obvious one is that the first subjects of both movements share similar repeated-note accompaniments; however, what matters here is not the mere fact but what Mozart achieves with it. Specifically, he keeps bringing it back as part of his larger scheme to emphasize the music's refusal to leave the home key despite repeated attempts by other themes in the exposition to do so.

In the C Major Quintet, as I have already noted, Mozart creates this impression by writing a huge first-subject group that has room for several repetitions of its initial idea, while in the much more concise G Minor Quintet (as mentioned in chapter 2), he begins his second subject with a new theme, but over the same accompaniment and in the same original key. The result in the former work is a feeling of stability and good cheer; in the latter work, the music paces like a caged animal increasingly desperate to escape confinement. The expressive effects may be totally opposite, but the means of achieving them are essentially identical, because the fundamental formal principle at work—that of delaying the establishment of the exposition's complimentary key for as long as possible—is the same in both cases.

Rather than focusing on questions of form, however, when you listen to this movement (accompanying CD track 6), pay particular attention to the shape and direction of the melodies themselves. One of the keys to getting the most out of classical music lies in broadening your conception of a musical idea beyond that of "the tune," and what makes this particular movement so powerful is that all of its most important melodies, even though the notes and rhythms are different, have a similar basic shape.

Namely, they consist of repeated short motives containing rising phrases immediately contradicted by falling ones. The effect produced by these repeated motives and symmetrical shapes resembles that of a nervous person wringing his hands, a trapped feeling heightened by the stabbing repeated-note accompaniments.

The first movement's anxiety is not ameliorated in the ensuring minuet. The angular melodies and stabbing accents only serve to heighten the tension in a way that the musical world would not see again until the symphonies of Mahler more than a hundred years later. Certainly no one would dream of dancing to this music, even though Mozart preserves the basic rhythm and form of a typical minuet. As with the similar movement in the G Minor Symphony K. 550, there's something deeply disturbing in the contrast between the movement's formal simplicity and its expressive angst. The reason for the minuet's harshness becomes clear at the opening of the slow movement, arguably the saddest piece that Mozart ever wrote. Perhaps the most important thing to notice, aside from the beauty and benumbed calm of the melodies themselves, is the fact that Mozart directs that the players use mutes, which gives the string timbres a hauntingly soft, veiled quality.

The finale of this quartet has come in for some criticism from those who insist that the only true art is miserable art. Had Mozart attempted a movement superficial in expression and flaccid in construction, this complaint might have some foundation, but in fact the way that he sets up his happy ending is both remarkable and logical. After three of the darkest movements that he ever wrote, Mozart begins the finale a shade darker still: the first violin sings an anguished lament in slow tempo. This melody is quite remarkable. It goes on for several minutes, but has no internal repetition and therefore no possibility of ever ending. In fact, there is no way to integrate such a tune into the wider framework of a sonata structure at all, and so Mozart doesn't even try. The violin winds down, stops, the key switches to the major, and the finale takes off at quick tempo, completely ignoring what has come before. What other, non-miserable solution could there be?

This finale also demonstrates very graphically the difference between Mozart's quartet and quintet styles. There's simply no way that he would have begun any movement in his quartets with an introduction such as this. It's too long, too extravagant, too centered on a single solo instrument, and its entire reason for existence hangs on its being unsuited to further development. It does, however, represent a sort of apotheosis of Mozart's vocally oriented style of instrumental writing, and it also opens the door to the kind of "let it all hang out" emotionalism that made Mozart one of the forerunners of musical romanticism.

String Quintet in D Major, K. 593 (1790)

This sunny and good-natured work is the most intellectual of the four string quintets under consideration, which means that some of its most interesting features involve aspects of form and development, rather than just the music's emotional character. There's nothing arcane or obscure about this; in fact, as with the quartets, when Mozart wants to make a purely musical point, he goes about it in the most direct way possible. Take the first movement: it begins with a slow introduction featuring a little rising rhythmic figure in the solo cello answered by the remaining players. This pattern repeats itself several times and leads to a quick main section. There's no need to worry about first and second subjects here. What matters most is that the themes of this allegro are constructed from all kinds of different rhythms, and this gives the music a delightfully tipsy quality quite at odds with the solemnity of the introduction.

Mozart's purpose becomes clear when, after the recapitulation, he brings back the slow introduction by way of a coda, only to close the movement as abruptly (and identically) as the exposition ended originally. It's curiously open-ended, but once again what follows sheds light on what was just heard. The slow movement is in full sonata form. Its first subject, like that of the first movement, has a very marked rhythmic structure, and the entire development section consists of a restatement of this opening theme, during which its second half, with its striking, jerky rhythm, rises to a passionate climax as it passes through the various instruments. The second subject is even more interesting, because it contains a much-repeated rhythmic motive clearly related to the little cello solo that opened the entire work. So this slow movement seems to have a dual function, both as contrast to and continued development of some of the most important characteristics of the first movement.

Having offered such a learned and tightly wound first half of the quintet, Mozart relaxes considerably from here on. The smoothly flowing minuet encloses a charming trio based on rising *arpeggios* (the notes of a chord stated in succession) over a light pizzicato accompaniment. For the finale Mozart returns to hunting rhythm (6/8 time), but at a blistering tempo that keeps the music bustling along like a spinning top, save for some genuinely funny pauses in the opening theme bound to elicit a laugh (or at least a smile) from unstuffy listeners. All of Mozart's skill goes into keeping this, one of his shortest finales (about five minutes with repeats), whizzing by with inexorable energy. What began as one of Mozart's most formally imaginative pieces ends with a movement expressive of little beyond the physical pleasure of exhilarating forward momentum.

String Quintet in E-flat Major, K. 614 (1791)

Mozart's last chamber work but one is also one of his most concise, perhaps reflecting the fact that even more than the quartets that Mozart dedicated to his friend Haydn, this work actually sounds very much like the older composer. Since the exact circumstances of composition are not known, there's no obvious explanation for this fact, although the work may have been intended for the same violinist (Johann Tost) to whom Haydn dedicated some of his quartets. Nor does Mozart need to apologize for paying yet another tribute to his best friend and the man universally acknowledged as the world's greatest living composer (although as I mentioned, Haydn thought that title belonged to Mozart). What are these Hayndesque elements?

1. The light compound meter (another 6/8 "hunt") for the first movement, very often found in Haydn, and the ubiquitous motivic development of the opening gesture presented by the two violas. Indeed, despite the fact that Mozart gives listeners a clear contrasting tune as his second subject (violin followed by cello), it's that opening motive that dominates to such an extent that one might call this exposition monothematic, as are many of Haydn's.

2. Mozart begins the second movement with a gentle nursery-rhyme theme and treats it to several charmingly witty variations, none of which obscure the theme to any measurable degree. Once again, Haydn was the acknowledged master of variation-form slow movements.

3. The opening theme of the minuet has a decidedly Haydnesque "kick" to its opening phrase, although the chromatic scales in the second half are pure Mozart. On the other hand, the trio is a *ländler,* the folk-dance precursor to the waltz, and it

comes very close to actually quoting the trio of the minuet of Haydn's Symphony No. 88.

4. The finale begins with a typical Haydn rondo theme and even tosses in a couple of the older composer's favorite jokes, including the "we can't remember how the tune goes" trick in the movement's later stages. On the other hand, the brilliant contrapuntal development section builds on the fascination with polyphonic writing that Mozart already explored with such virtuosity in the "Jupiter" Symphony of three years earlier.

In short (and since this quintet is so concise, I will be too), this piece represents a characterful mixture of personal and borrowed elements, but one must take care to understand that the act of borrowing implies no lack of originality or inspiration. When Mozart (like all great composers) borrows, he always borrows well, and whatever he chooses to use is invariably the right thing in its proper place.

Clarinet Quintet in A Major, K. 581 (1789)

I discuss the first movement of this glorious work (accompanying CD track 5) extensively in "What Makes Mozart Sound Like Mozart?" and in considering the remaining three movements, I want to focus on one element in particular, which is very revealing of Mozart's style and of the classical style in general and as it was also practiced by Haydn and Beethoven in their own chamber music.

Writing a clarinet quintet isn't easy, for the simple reason that the contrast in timbre between the single woodwind and the string quartet naturally means that the clarinet will always sound like a soloist, just as a singer can't possible "accompany" a violin. The ear simply refuses to accept what it recognizes as nonsense. This suits Mozart, the composer of exquisitely vocal-sounding instrumental music, just fine, but it's a real pain if an important consideration is balance and equality of voices in a chamber music setting. This last quality may not seem terribly important, but any work lasting half an hour and consisting entirely of solo anything over an unvarying accompaniment (especially one as inherently homogeneous as a string quartet) will prove aurally fatiguing in very short order. On the other hand, Mozart cannot restrain the clarinet to the point where listeners wonder why he bothered to include one in the first place. How does he escape this dilemma in the work's remaining three movements?

The larghetto second movement, in sonata form without development, naturally has two subject groups, but Mozart conceives both as duets. The first subject pits the clarinet against the cello, while the second features clarinet and first violin. Thus, one method Mozart adopts involves presenting the clarinet with another instrument, either simultaneously (that is, in counterpoint) or in close dialogue. In the third movement, he takes a more sequential approach specifically adapted to the form of the minuet. As mentioned previously, this particular example has two trio sections. In the first trio, the clarinet pauses completely, only to return as soloist in the second. One can clearly see how the form (in this case, the addition of the extra trio) is dictated specifically by the requirements of the ensemble. The same holds true for the finale, which is a set of variations on a typically childlike theme (in two halves, both repeated). Here's how the individual variations lay out:

Theme: Stated by the strings with the clarinet coloring the ends of phrases only (exactly the same treatment of strings and winds as in the variation finale of Piano Concerto No. 17, CD track 4).

Variation 1: Solo clarinet decorates the theme in the strings.

Variation 2: The first violin leads, later becoming a duet with clarinet in both halves of the theme.

Variation 3: The viola leads (first violin in the second half), with a very modest contribution from the clarinet at the end of each half.

Variation 4: A brilliant series of trade-offs between clarinet and first violin, with a touch of songful clarinet atop the chattering violin at the beginning of the second half.

Variation 5: A short bridge passage leads to a lovely adagio, also a duet in alternating phrases between clarinet and violin.

Coda: Strings and clarinet take turns sharing the tune in a quicker tempo.

I have purposely refrained from characterizing the music expres-sively. That happy discovery I leave to you, and I hope that when you hear the complete work, you will not just find additional pleasure in what Mozart has to say, but will also relish the manner in which he says it.

Adagio and Rondo in C Minor, K. 617, for Flute, Oboe, Viola, Cello, and Glass Harmonica (1791)

C all it a little "extra credit" if you will, but I include this, Mozart's final chamber work, because in its modest way, it really does sum up everything that needs to be said about that special quality of intimate conversation that remains the chamber music medium's crowning glory. A glass harmonica is a set of drinking glasses tuned by being filled with water, played by rubbing moistened fingertips around the rims. I am sure I'm not the only one with a certain amount of youthful personal experience with the most primitive form of this instrument, namely, fiddling with the wine glasses at various formal functions such as weddings, bar mitzvahs, confirmations, and so forth. The glass harmonica itself was supposedly perfected, if not necessarily invented, by none other than Benjamin Franklin.

Mozart apparently knew the instrument from his early travels to London, but the work under consideration resulted from his encounter with Marianne Kirchgässner, a blind traveling glass harmonica virtuoso (really) with apparently quite a fine reputation, since many composers of the day wrote for her. Mozart's contribution to her legacy consists of two pieces: a short solo adagio (misleadingly numbered K. 356) and this quintet. What marks this piece as special is the fact that Mozart was freely able to choose the ensemble he thought most appropriate to partner the glass harmonica. Knowing what we do about his desire to achieve maximum expressive results through balance and equality between voices in classical chamber music, I invite you to listen and share Mozart's obvious delight in composing what remains to this day the single, solitary masterwork featuring one of history's great instrumental curiosities.

Music for Wind Ensemble (Harmonienmusik)

Serenade No. 10 in B-flat Major, K. 361
   ("Gran Partita") (1781?)
Serenade No. 11 in E-flat Major, K. 375 (1781)
Serenade No. 12 in C Minor, K. 388 (1782–3)

Vast quantities of music for wind ensemble were composed in the classical period, although no one is quite sure why the little group known in German as the *Harmonie* became so popular. It could have been a fad. Once one nobleman let it be known that he wouldn't go anywhere without his wind sextet (pairs of oboes, bassoons and horns; clarinets were added later), everyone else had to follow suit. It could also be that the ready availability of a superb pool of wind players (a Bohemian specialty still very much alive today, as you can hear for yourself in any number of recordings and performances from the Czech Republic) made maintaining this mini-orchestra a cheap way to demonstrate the "culture" of an illustrious but otherwise down-and-out noble house.

We also tend to forget these days that the first purpose of the nobility was not to lazily take advantage of peasants and live lavishly. They were soldiers dedicated (when they were not fighting each other) to protecting the residents of their own region and also, if called upon, to support their king or emperor. The military establishments that they maintained necessarily included wind players, trumpeters, and drummers (when a composer needed timpani, he requisitioned them from the local armory and not from an instrument-rental agency), who played the "outdoors music" necessary to assist in regimental maneuvers. From this it would certainly have been a short step to having these same players entertain their commanders at table, provide some dance music, or fill the leisure hours with arrangements of greatest hits from popular operas (including Mozart's). After all, the musicians were already on payroll—whether serving in the actual military establishment or as part of the household staff.

The above three works represent the cream of Mozart's considerable crop of wind ensemble music and stand at the very summit of the repertoire. As the extensive discussion so far of chamber music has provided a firm foundation in what to expect as regards both form and content, a brief description of each of these pieces (combined with the experience of CD track 10) will give you a good basic grounding in this very rewarding and sadly neglected musical backwater.

I mentioned in my discussion of Mozart's personal style ("What Makes Mozart Sound Like Mozart?") that among composers who were "generalists," he had a very special feeling for wind instruments and usually wrote for as many as he could get his hands on when it came to orchestral music. Perhaps the most important thing to keep in mind about his writing for winds, aside from its expressive, vocal quality, is that Mozart makes no concessions to the players in terms of emotional depth, formal sophistication, and ensemble technique in the music he writes for them. This is possibly the principal requirement for the creation of any truly great work, for if, say, you have to write for two lousy oboists and so neglect them as much as possible or simplify their parts, the result will be a piece that cannot avoid pandering to the lowest common denominator, and it will certainly limit the music's expressive range. Mozart would make concessions to local circumstances of performance in terms of the ensembles he had to work with, but with remarkably few exceptions, he expected the highest musical standards from his performers at all times.

The work that illustrates this best is the Serenade in C Minor, which later became the String Quintet in the same key. Having four movements, like a symphony, and set in an anguished minor tonality, there's nothing "light" about this music. Compared to the string-quintet version, this octet (pairs of oboes, clarinets, horns, and bassoons) sounds fuller, more colorful, and vastly more evil. Nothing conveys a devilish sneer in music quite like woodwind trills, such as those at the opening of the first move-ment. The minuet is canonic (various instruments follow the tune as in a round), and the timbre of the winds makes the imitative entries clearer than the more homogeneous tone of string instru-ments. Lastly, in the finale (which is a theme and variations), the contrast is much greater with wind instruments between the initial statement of the movement's gaunt, minor-key theme and the cartoonlike high spirits of its major-key transformation at the very end.

The Serenade in E-flat Major stands in a similar relationship to its C minor cousin, as do the String Quintets in C Major and G Minor. Written for the same distribution of eight players, this ebullient work also shows no sign of being on a small scale. It has five movements (two minuets), and a finale with a particularly tangy opening theme. As with the String Quintet in C Major, Mozart demonstrates his intention to take his time and "write big" in the opening movement, which has great breadth and a genuinely regal, processional quality with the Mozart rhythm quite prominent. You might also notice that the second minuet is much livelier than the more graceful and courtly first one, thus avoiding any suggestion of monotony.

Monotony is hardly an issue with respect to the "Gran Partita," K. 361. A certain atmosphere of mystery hovers over this fifty-minute extravaganza, written for an ensemble consisting of two oboes, two clarinets, two basset horns (lower members of the clarinet family), four horns, two bassoons, and double bass or contrabassoon. The sonority of this collection of players is impossible to describe verbally: adjectives such as *succulent, juicy, plush, burnished,* and *fruity* come to mind, but you will notice that the emphasis on middle and lower registers (no flutes, for example) greatly enhances the music's smoothness and timbral warmth. With so many instruments to exploit, the coloristic possibilities are virtually unlimited, and Mozart seems determined to take advantage of every single one of them.

The "Gran Partita" (the nickname isn't Mozart's) has seven movements, including two minuets (both with two trios). As in the E-flat Serenade, the second is more energetic than the first. Of the two slow movements, the first is the one that drove Antonio Salieri crazy with jealousy at the beginning of the film *Amadeus.* In keeping with the more relaxed character of a serenade, both slow movements are in simple ABA form. Mozart calls the second one a *romanze,* and its B section is an allegretto in a stern minor key. Its quicker tempo gives the music an anxious character that demonstrates once again that for Mozart, the serenade style, while less rigorous formally, never precludes intensity of emotional expression.

The sixth movement is a very expansive theme and six variations, each one of which features differing combinations of instruments:

Theme: In two parts, both repeated, and both halves led off by the clarinets.

Variation 1: Oboes and basset horns.

Variation 2: Clarinets, basset horns, and bassoons.

Variation 3: Everyone begins, then the music breaks up into a series of duets between clarinets (primarily), oboes, and bassoons.

Variation 4: A short variation for full ensemble led by clarinets and bassoons.

Variation 5: A lovely adagio for solo oboe over a variety of flowing accompaniments in basset horns and clarinets, with gentle support from the remaining players.

Variation 6: Everyone participates, but the tune belongs to the first oboe and first basset horn, joined in the second half by their partners as well as the two clarinets.

Mozart sandwiches the five inner movements between a sonata-form opening and rondo finale. The opening movement begins with a stately introduction that features the Mozart rhythm, as does much of the ensuing allegro. The exposition is largely mono-thematic: that is, the opening theme dominates the entire section and there really isn't a clearly defined "second-subject group" of themes at all. The finale, in contrast to the first movement's stateliness, is that zany celebration of wind sonority on track 10 of the accompanying CD. Listening to the heavenly first slow movement (adagio), it's easy to understand why Mozart's contemporaries (except Haydn of course) might have wished their young rival dead.

No one knows for whom Mozart wrote this remarkable work, exactly when he wrote it (estimates range from 1781 to 1784), or even if the whole thing was ever played in his lifetime—hence the "mystery" referred to above. The sketchy information that we possess confirms only performances of a selection of movements, but it's very unlikely that Mozart would have written such a massive piece and invested such care in its composition had he not intended it for an appropriately significant musical occasion. Doubtless the truth would, as ever, turn out to be quite mundane, but somehow it seems more appropriate to leave this particular example of the Mozart myth—that of the solitary, misunderstood genius writing huge, complicated works destined to be misunderstood by the shallow Viennese aristocracy of the day—intact for the time being. Let's just agree, as we draw our survey of Mozart's greatest chamber music to a close with this lavish and truly one-of-a-kind example, that even if some of his contemporaries did misunderstand him, there's nothing in the music that says that we have to as well.

Part 3

Orchestral Music

Introduction

The history of the orchestra in the classical period parallels that of chamber music very closely, at least to the extent that over the course of Mozart's career, one sees the same gradual emancipation of large ensembles from dependence on the baroque continuo, just as occurred with smaller groupings. One practical consequence of this is that orchestras enjoyed the possibility of growing larger. In the baroque period, the need to find some semblance of balance (not to be confused with equality; the continuo always maintained a clearly subservient position) between the larger ensemble and tiny continuo group meant that most orchestras were necessarily quite small—just a handful or strings, with maybe a couple of oboes. Any additional instruments assumed the role of soloists, like singers in an opera. The principal orchestral form during this time, therefore, was the concerto—a work for solo instrument(s) and orchestra, and the forms of the baroque concerto were essentially the same as those of the opera aria.

Having more instruments on hand, however, obviously allowed composers to provide more colorfully inflected melodies and accompaniments, and it also meant that, as with chamber music, a new kind of orchestral writing was possible, in which the various players acted as soloists, as part of the accompaniment, and in every conceivable combination in between. Concertos remained very important during the classical period, but alongside them the symphony became the orchestral medium of choice. What orchestras lack in finesse and rhythmic suppleness (as compared to chamber ensembles), they more than make up for in dynamic range, color, and sheer power. As you may well imagine, these qualities fit the narrative and dramatic sonata style perfectly, and this once again raises the interesting issue (but not so interesting that we need to deal with it here) of the extent to which form influences the development of a medium, or the medium influences the rise of a new form.

Even in Mozart's day, however, maintaining an orchestra was an expensive operation. There were no independent ensembles of the variety familiar to us now: either publicly subsidized (as in Europe) or not-for-profit performing arts institutions (as in the USA). Orchestras were either pick-up groups organized by a composer or impresario for a specific series of concerts, or else they were the employees of the great noble houses. In both cases they were, by today's standards, still quite small. A private orchestra might, on a particularly splendid occasion, gather together a couple of dozen players; larger groups for public concerts could double that number for a limited time. The roster of players and available instruments varied widely from town to town, estate to estate—and there was no standardization at all. Mozart could usually count on, at a minimum, strings plus horns and oboes in pairs, often with a pair of bassoons too. Flutes (one or two) were relatively common, trumpets and drums (almost always appearing together) much less so, and clarinets were a comparatively new invention. Additional percussion was used only for "special effects," such as evocations of battles or military marches.

Mozart's output for orchestra varies much more widely in quality than his chamber music does for just this reason. He could never be sure what conditions he would find and the extent to

which these might "cramp his style." You have already seen that
Mozart invariably tried to get the most lavish forces that he could,
particularly with respect to his woodwind sections, and one can
get some idea of the prevailing state of affairs by recalling Haydn's
famous suggestion that in order to perform his very grand and
technically challenging late symphonies, it might be a good idea
to have at least *one* rehearsal before the concert. Make no mistake: that doesn't mean that conditions were dreadful. Rather,
the caliber of most orchestral players must have been similar to
that of, say, Broadway pit musicians today. They were trained to
read just about anything at sight and at least turn in an honorable
professional effort most of the time.

However, for this same reason, the style of orchestral writing in the classical period tended toward a certain degree of
standardization. Composers anxious to assert their originality
did so at their peril, since they were completely at the mercy of
local conditions once the music left their hands. Difficult passages
would simply be rewritten or cut, special instruments omitted,
and movements reordered or even replaced entirely (sometimes
with music by others). At a time when most performers were
also composers, some of them very good ones (and copyright
protection was unheard of), rather amazing things could happen
to any musical work.

The case of Haydn's symphonies was special in that he had
at his disposal his own personally trained orchestra with which
to experiment. However even these works inevitably reveal the
influence of local conditions, and an entire school of composers
made a living writing "fake Haydn," often passing it off as the real
thing. Mozart, gifted as he was, similarly understood the value of
a good imitation, as you will see in the discussion of his Symphony
No. 25, the "Little G Minor." Haydn, in any case, just happened
to be in a position such that most of the conditions under which

he worked in his lifetime were favorable to his artistic inclinations and skills, as he was the first person to admit.

Mozart, who had little such luck before moving permanently to Vienna, was often content to turn out breezy, entertaining pieces on demand in various shapes and styles, without any obvious or overwhelming originality as regards either form or content. Naturally some of these (mostly early) pieces are very well made, but quite a few survive to reach occasional modern performance only because they have the name "Mozart" attached to them. Indeed, some are so stylistically anonymous that their authorship is open to question. Such was the case for many years with Symphony No. 37: only the slow introduction is by Mozart, while the rest is the work of Michael Haydn (Joseph's younger brother and a Salzburg colleague of Mozart's father).

Mozart's concertos, on the other hand, were mostly written for his own concerts (or those of his colleagues), at which he conducted a hand-picked orchestra from the keyboard, and so their quality is correspondingly higher and more consistent when taken as a whole. The numbers speak for themselves: of Mozart's sixty-odd symphonies, only six postdate his move to Vienna in 1781, while during the same period, he produced fourteen of his twenty-seven piano concertos. Mozart simply wasn't in demand as a composer of symphonies, but when it came to piano concertos, he had essentially a wide-open field in which to update the form in terms of the classical sonata style, just as Haydn turned the old baroque overture or *sinfonia* into a new and exciting type of orchestral work called a symphony. Taken together, however, Mozart's best symphonies, concertos, overtures, and serenades comprise as rich and significant body of work for orchestra as that of any composer in history.

Serenades

"Haffner" Serenade in D Major, K. 250 (1776)
"Posthorn" Serenade in D Major, K. 320 (1779)
Eine Kleine Nachtmusik, K. 525 (1787)

Mozart is just about the only composer of orchestral serenades in the classical period whose works in this form are still valued. Most pieces of this type were written for special occasions and thus performed only a single time, so for the composer it didn't pay to lavish too much time and attention on them, even when the event in question was particularly important or grand. On the other hand, the opportunity to write acres of music using every player he could get his hands on was bound to catch him in top form on at least a few occasions, and I offer three of these for your consideration.

It's a little difficult to pin down exactly how many symphonies and serenades Mozart actually wrote, as their relationship is a bit incestuous. For example, the symphony K. 248c consists of the first, sixth, fifth, and eighth movements (in that order) of the "Haffner" Serenade with a new timpani part, while the "Haffner" Symphony (No. 35, K. 385) is all that is left of a second serenade that Mozart composed for the same Haffner family whose wedding celebrations resulted in the original commission for K. 250. Well, almost all that is left—there's a march hanging around in old Köchel's catalogue somewhere and the symphony version had extra wind parts added, but I don't need to get into that discussion. You get the point.

There's also no crucial difference worth noting (formally speaking) between works called *serenade, partita, divertimento, cassation, notturno,* or any of a number of similar names in various languages. All basically mean the same thing: a light piece with extra movements in simple forms (such as minuets and rondos), designed to entertain listeners at special festivities or events for any amount of time up to an hour or more. Even *Eine Kleine Nachtmusik,* often celebrated as the four-movement "pocket symphony" par excellence, enjoys that reputation only because its original second movement, an additional minuet, is missing.

If you listen to the energetic and festive opening movements of the "Haffner" and "Posthorn" serenades, you may notice something surprising: for all their vigorous trumpeting and drumming, for all the rushing strings and dabs of wind color, they contain few distinctive tunes at all. This raises an issue very important in understanding the classical style, one that these deliberately "light" works help put in its proper context. Festive music such as is found here isn't always supposed to be emotionally profound. It's designed to sound cheerful and impress the listener with its brilliance—like a display of fireworks—and so these movements consist almost entirely of fanfares, vigorous rhythms, and tiny melodic cells arranged in ear-catching succession, with nary a shred of that broad melody for which Mozart is so famous.

Actually, this sort of musical construction is very common. You've already seen Mozart use one type of it in the finale of the String Quartet in A Major, K. 464, which is built almost entirely on a tiny descending four-note chromatic scale. His use of this technique also characterizes much of the first movement of the "Jupiter" Symphony, and accounts for its ceremonial pomp. However, when a large piece of music lacks tunes, it tends to be classified as intellectual in character, which usually means inexpressive, and lacking in emotion or the sort of surface appeal that clearly articulated, memorable melodies so readily convey.

This isn't entirely fair. When Mozart writes in this particular fashion, one can plainly see that the resultant emphasis on the grandeur of an entire movement, rather than on the distinctive qualities of its individual thematic elements, has the same aesthetic point as does the fact that the beauty of, say, an Egyptian pyramid lies primarily in its whole form rather than in the individual attractiveness of the blocks of stone from which it's built. More importantly, Mozart's personal style exists just as distinctively in music where color, rhythm, and shape assert themselves without the mediating services of important or unusually distinctive themes.

"Haffner" Serenade in D Major, K. 250 (1776)

Played with the March in D Major, K. 249, that Mozart wrote as entrance and exit music, the "Haffner" Serenade is his longest orchestral work, lasting about seventy minutes. Without the march it still takes an hour or so and remains the longest orchestral serenade by any composer that we care about. It has eight—count 'em!—eight movements, including two andantes, one "official" rondo (the second andante is also in rondo form), three minuets, and a big opening and finale, both framed by extensive introductions. In addition, movements 2–4 form a miniature violin concerto, but in keeping with the serenade's relaxing character, their order (andante, minuet, rondo) means that there's no intellectual sonata movement at all included in the concerto sequence, and this in turn gives it the character of an episode or subset of the larger work.

The orchestration includes pairs of flutes, oboes, bassoons, trumpets, and horns, with timpani and the usual strings. Rather than review each movement in turn, let me give you a few pointers that illustrate how Mozart wrings the maximum amount of color and variety from the various forms, styles, and instruments at his disposal.

1. All three minuets are quite different. The first one (third movement) surprises listeners by being in a stern minor key, but the carefree trio's solo violin serves a dual function as the second of the concerto movements as well. The second minuet (fifth movement) is marked *menuetto galante,* which means that Mozart gives it a very pompous and stately quality at a moderate tempo. The last minuet (seventh movement) has two trios, making particularly effective use of the wind instruments.
2. Mozart's writing for woodwinds reveals typical care. Oboes play in the first movement, flutes take over for the next three (the concerto), oboes return for the next two, flutes play in the seventh movement, and oboes are back for the finale (mirroring the first movement). It would not have been unusual in Mozart's time for these parts to be played by the same musicians (unheard of today), versatility being an additional guarantor of employment, so we might actually be seeing Mozart making a virtue of necessity.
3. Trumpets and timpani play in movements 1 and 8 only.
4. Trumpets without timpani play in movements 5 and 7 only (some performances add timpani parts anyway).

Even though this loose arrangement of movements shows Mozart concerned to keep things aurally interesting, don't feel any obligation to listen to this work all the way through at a sitting. Certainly the Haffners and their guests were free to talk, move about, and come and go as they pleased. Mozart expected it, and his job was to present his listeners with something worth hearing to the extent that they felt like paying attention, so there's no reason why you should treat the music any differently. Besides, just as the best wine for cooking is a bottle that you wouldn't be ashamed to serve at the dinner table, the best background music should always be something that stands on its own merits and would be delightful in the foreground too.

"Posthorn" Serenade in D Major, K. 320 (1779)

Orchestration: flautino (piccolo or small recorder), 2 flutes, 2 oboes, 2 bassoons, 2 horns, posthorn, 2 trumpets, timpani, strings.

This is arguably Mozart's most colorful large orchestral work, not just for the unusually varied assortment of instruments that it contains, but also in the way that they are used. Not only does it mark a huge stylistic advance on the "Haffner" Serenade of a few years earlier, it pretty much outclasses all of the symphonies, save the last six that Mozart composed after his move to Vienna. As has been seen time and time again, Mozart was one of those artists who liked to paint on a broad canvas, and his dullest works tend to be the smaller ones, since they have little time to do anything else but assert his remarkable sense of symmetry and proportion, whereas larger works allow him to fill up their grander movements and sections with all kinds of ear-catching and interesting detail and to vary the color, size, and shape of his musical ideas in surprising and unexpected ways.

This is exactly what happens in this seven-movement extravaganza lasting some forty-five minutes. It opens grandly with a typical question-and-answer formula, with each question consisting of nothing more than the Mozart rhythm for full orchestra. After merely six measures (three questions and answers), the movement takes off like a shot, and as already mentioned, its pageantry finds little room for extended melody. Even so, in comparing the first movements of these two serenades, it's clear that the later work packs even more variety and rhythmic energy into its phrases. It's also worth noting that this movement contains no large sectional repeats, here signifying a less rigorous formal organization appropriate to the character of a serenade.

The short second-movement minuet, with its stately outer sections and gently flowing trio, tames some of the first movement's manic energy on the way to one of Mozart's most delicious creations, the *concertante*. This term, obviously related to the concerto, simply means either: (1) the presence of concerto elements—that is, formal instrumental solos—in a work not called a concerto, or (2) a symphonic work featuring two or more soloists (often called in such cases *symphony concertante*). Here the soloists are two flutes and two oboes (with a little help from the two bassoons). The tempo is *andante grazioso* (moderate walking tempo) and the opening tune delightfully witty: a sort of march around the poultry yard. It is both rustic and sophisticated at the same time, rather like Marie Antoinette dressing up as a farm girl in her "authentic" peasant play-village behind Versailles.

Perhaps the French analogy contains a grain of truth, since the magic continues in the fourth movement, which goes by its French name of *rondeau*. The sheer amount of charm Mozart generates simply by manipulating the intertwining of pairs of flutes and oboes staggers the imagination, although of course having terrific tunes never hurts. What happens next, however, takes the concertante concept to a new level. Two bassoons replace the two flutes as soloists, and Mozart gives listeners one of his most richly expressive minor-key slow movements, its sadness deepened and made palpable by the gorgeously long melodic lines given to the wind soloists. Notice the difference between the "Haffner" Serenade, where the minor key comes and goes quickly in the first minuet, and here, where it serves to provide the emotional core of the piece, and also how Mozart uses this less soloistic "quasi-concertante" to ease listeners back into the main body of the serenade.

This is usually the place for some observation about how remarkable it is that Mozart wrote such profound music for "mere entertainment," but the fact is that all music is mere entertainment, and great music is even greater entertainment. What one witnesses in works such as the "Posthorn" Serenade is Mozart's understanding not just of this basic fact but (and this is where the genius part comes in) his ability to write at such a consistently high level of inspiration no matter what the occasion or circumstances.

Trumpets and drums return in the sixth movement, another bold minuet that, like many of the extra dance movements in Mozart's larger works, has two trio sections. The first features the flautino, or at least we think it does, because although Mozart mentions it in his score and leaves space for it on the page, he didn't write the actual part. Most performances simply have it double the melody in the first violins, which it does charmingly. The second trio features the famous posthorn (it sounds like a darker-toned bugle) that gives the entire work its nickname—unfairly as it turns out when you consider that it plays for scarcely a minute. Still, the added color is quite special and very surprising in this context.

The finale, four minutes of unrestrained high spirits, has more clear-cut tunes than does the first movement. The absence of an exposition repeat or of extensive development once again signals Mozart's determination to write music of generally relaxed character. Taken as a whole, it's easy to imagine that Mozart had a terrific time writing this—grand entertainment, which was (and I've intentionally saved this tidbit for last) most likely commissioned like most of his larger serenades for the summer graduation festivities at Salzburg U.

Eine Kleine Nachtmusik, K. 525 (1787)

The *Nachtmusik* of the title is simply German for notturno, which, as already seen, is synonymous with serenade. Originally in five movements (one of its two minuets is lost) and composed for string quintet (two violins, viola, cello, and bass), but familiar today as played by a fuller string ensemble, this is the work that for many listeners means "Mozart." Stephen Sondheim named one of his most popular musicals after it; comedian P. D. Q. Bach (Peter Schickele) made fun of it; generations of music apprecia-tion students have learned sonata form from it; and Tom Skerrit in his role as Captain Dallas enjoyed a relaxing moment with its second movement, Romance, shortly before being eaten by the creature in the film *Alien.* You really can't get more famous than that.

The first movement, with that instantly memorable introduc-tory fanfare in the shape of a typically Mozartean "up and down" melodic arch, really could serve as the perfect introduction to sonata form for textbooks: it has an exposition with a clear first subject; an even clearer second subject; a pellucidly clear development section based entirely on the second subject; and an iridescently, preternaturally clear recapitulation, in which all of the tunes reappear with punctual regularity in their proper order. In short, it reveals a formal stiffness found almost nowhere in Mozart's mature work at all, and one far more typical of the early symphonies and other pieces composed on a similarly small scale.

But there's a big difference between, say, K. 97 and K. 525. That difference can be summed up in one word: tunes. Each movement of *Eine Kleine Nachtmusik* contains an abundance of sweet, ravishing, witty, songful melody. This is the bane of music theorists, because, try as they might, there is no accepted way to analyze melodies in order to describe why some strike listeners as instantly memorable and expressive while others pass by without attracting any notice at all. Mozart's combination of wonderful tunes placed within the confines of extremely regular, ideally proportioned form (in all four movements) both fulfills the music's promise as a "little serenade" and instinctively conveys to even casual listeners the exquisite craftsmanship characteristic of all great miniatures.

This is truly all that you need to know. Indeed, it's just about all we *can* know, since the historical details concerning the origin of a work that so many listeners regard as the very embodiment of classical perfection in sound have yet to be discovered.

Symphonies

Symphony No. 25 in G Minor, K. 183 (1773)
Symphony No. 29 in A Major, K. 201 (1774)
Symphony No. 31 in D Major, K. 297 ("Paris") (1778)
Symphony No. 35 in D Major, K. 385 ("Haffner") (1782)
Symphony No. 36 in C Major, K. 425 ("Linz") (1783)
Symphony No. 38 in D Major, K. 504 ("Prague") (1786)
Symphony No. 39 in E-flat Major, K. 543 (1788)
Symphony No. 40 in G Minor, K. 550 (1788)
Symphony No. 41 in C Major, K. 551 ("Jupiter") (1788)

The fact that I am only considering nine out of more than sixty Mozart symphonies is not as surprising as the numbers alone might indicate. When Mozart died in 1791, his older colleague and best friend Joseph Haydn was in London writing the first set of twelve symphonies (Nos. 94–104) that, alongside the six "Paris" Symphonies (Nos. 82–87) and assisted more than a little by his pupil Beethoven a decade or so later, would go on to make the symphony the premiere genre of orchestral music. But in 1791 all that was in the future. For most of Mozart's career, the symphony was more aptly described by its equally common designation: overture.

Public concerts in Mozart's day tended to be long—several hours at a stretch. Then, as now to a very large extent, the featured performers were vocal and instrumental soloists, and the genres of choice were arias and concertos. Symphonies provided light curtain raisers, musical interludes between more important items, and zippy finales at the end of the evening. Often a work's several movements might be spread over the entire event or used to bracket other pieces many minutes, or even hours, apart. Mozart was aware of the symphony's potential in the hands of a composer like Haydn, and as in the chamber music, one can hear him progress clearly from admiration and imitation to mature mastery in a completely personal style.

Given this background, the fact that there are even half a dozen mature works that do rate being considered "main events" is something of a miracle. In discussing these nine works (and also the piano concertos later on), which may be said to summarize the best of Mozart's symphonic output at various stages in his career, I have prepared a table indicating the orchestration of each piece, listing all of the instruments required—aside from the standard string ensemble common to all. This will both save time in the discussion and facilitate easy comparison when listening.

More importantly, an accurate list of the instruments employed will always tell you as much about each work as any lengthy verbal description can. In the small classical orchestra, the impact made by a pair of, say, clarinets taking the place of the usual oboes (as in Symphony No. 39) can have a huge effect on the sound of the music. This is particularly true with a composer like Mozart, who always makes colorful use of the resources available to him and takes great pains to differentiate one work from another purely through his use of the orchestra. A prime example of this occurs in the second subject of the first movement of the "Linz" Symphony (No. 36), where the absence of both flutes and clarinets, instead of being a hindrance, leads Mozart to discover some particularly rich and juicy wind sonorities using oboes, bassoons, horns, and trumpets. It's a brief passage, over in a flash, but it's a distinct sound that you will hear in no other symphony by Mozart (or by anyone else for that matter).

This chart, then, offers a convenient point of entry into the world of each work, by directing your attention towards the particular forces that Mozart selects (or had no choice but to use) for each. Knowing what to listen for really is half the battle in coming to understand any great work of music well.

Symphony No.	Instruments in Addition to Strings						timpani (pairs)
	flutes	oboes	clarinets	bassoons	horns	trumpets	
25		2		2	4		
29		2			2		
31	2	2	2	2	2	2	1
35	2	2	2	2	2	2	1
36		2		2	2	2	1
38	2	2		2	2	2	1
39	1		2	2	2	2	1
40	1	2	(2)	2	2		
41	1	2		2	2	2	1

Symphony No. 25 in G Minor, K. 183 (1773)

This is one of a number of symphonies (not necessarily by Mozart) thought to have been inspired by Haydn's Symphony No. 39, which was quite famous in its day. Haydn's also has four horns and is in the key of G minor. Since this is one of only two symphonies by Mozart in a minor key, and the only other one (the famous No. 40) is also in G minor, this symphony has earned the nickname the "Little G Minor," even though, like so much of Mozart's best work, it really isn't so little, each of the four movements being in fact generously proportioned in comparison with many of the early symphonies.

Hearing the symphony now and comparing it to the great works to come, it's easy to spot its weaknesses. The first subject of the opening movement loses energy rather quickly as it becomes a plaintive oboe solo. Mozart was not the best imitator of Haydn's nervous and "twitchy" style: his music, as has been seen time and time again, thrives on long, lyrical lines and for that needs a certain symmetry of phrasing. The problem here is that the oboe tune not only dissipates the energetic opening, it's also arguably by far the most arresting, typically Mozartean moment in the entire movement. The transition to the second subject spends too much time getting there and switches abruptly (too abruptly?) to the major. Moreover its themes (also true of the slow movement) are not particularly interesting. Mozart's inimitable melodic style has not yet developed.

On the other hand, the short development section has plenty of power, and the lead-back to the recapitulation is one of those moments that justifies my suggestion that you have a look at the list of instruments and pay particular attention to the wind parts: the four horns make a magnificent crescendo launching the return of the first subject in dramatic fashion. Even here, in this early work, one sees Mozart adopting the custom of keeping the music in the tonic (home) minor key right up to the end, a prac-tice that effectively saves the movement from a possible charge of emotional schizophrenia, while at the same time allaying the suspicion that the opening minor-key first subject was merely a spot of local color.

The following slow movement has an attractively veiled qual-ity produced by having the violins muted (not an unusual effect for the period) even if the tunes aren't yet great Mozart, but the gaunt, minor-key minuet has a surprise in its trio: a marvelous woodwind sextet for two oboes, two bassoon, and two horns. Perhaps the best movement in the entire symphony, the finale is a concentrated essay in monothematic sonata form. The entire exposition is based on the opening theme, and its characteristic rhythm makes Mozart's variants particularly easy and rewarding to follow. So while it may not be perfect taken as a whole, there's a lot to be said for a work that gets better as it goes.

Symphony No. 29 in A Major, K. 201 (1774)

Always popular among musicians and audiences alike, this gentle symphony reveals much of the great composer to come. When one compares the first movements of this work and Symphony No. 25 of a year earlier, the progress that Mozart has made is little short of amazing. Consider the opening of Symphony No. 29: a rising sequence of softly sustained harmony. It could go on rising forever, but of course it doesn't, and what Mozart has learned is the secret of giving the impression of great breadth in a small space by varying the length and shape of his phrases and the rhythm and pace of his accompaniments, and by gathering tension as he proceeds rather than beginning in a frenzy and letting the energy gradually dissipate. In Symphony No. 25, the transition to the second subject is very long and full of protracted sequences and frantic rushing about. Here there is an actual transition theme—and a very pretty one too—that takes listeners much farther in a fraction of the time. Such is the power of Mozartean melody.

The slow movement, again with muted violins, is in sonata form. The development is episodic—that is, it consists of new material and so gives the movement the feel of a simple ABA form while actually being a bit more highly organized thanks to the expansive A sections, which are really sonata expositions. The melodies contrast the opening gentle march rhythms with typically gracious examples of Mozart's long-lined vocal style. You will notice that while the oboes and horns had no solos at all in the first movement, they have several here, particular at the very end when the gloves (meaning in this case the violin mutes) come off to surprising effect. The same march rhythms, only in quicker tempo, characterize the outer sections of the minuet, and again you hear short solos for the tiny wind section (but not in the trio, which features strings alone, save for a single held note in each half for the oboes and horns).

The breezy finale is another of those hunting movements in 6/8 time, such as the one met in Mozart's "Hunt" Quartet. Here, however, he has real horns, and he uses them with particular effectiveness in the transition between the movement's first and second subjects. Compare this passage of four-note phrases tossed between horns and violins to the transition in the first movement: Mozart has learned to give even his "utility music" thematic significance, and this greatly enriches the opportunities for contrast, color, and interesting development. It's not until the very end of the symphony, however, that Mozart allows the horns and oboes to really cut loose, with a brilliant fanfare that brings the work to a joyous conclusion. In this symphony, most of the elements of "great" Mozart are in place.

Symphony No. 31 in D Major, K. 297 ("Paris") (1778)

This work was composed during a trip to the French capital. Fortunately, the exact composition of the orchestra at its premier is known: twenty-two violins; five violas; eight cellos; five basses; pairs of flutes, oboes, and clarinets; four bassoons; six brass (the two horn parts were probably doubled); and timpani. Having been told that Parisians had no patience for long German-style symphonies, Mozart accordingly omitted the minuet completely and wrote the entire work without formal repeats, making this seventeen of the most concentrated minutes of music that he ever created. He also wrote a second slow movement when the director of the concerts expressed his dissatisfaction with the first one, and there is some controversy over which came first, although the standard choice is the movement that I will consider here.

All questions of form aside, the most important audible fact about the "Paris" Symphony is the large wind section, which as you may expect Mozart uses with enthusiasm. This is his first symphony to call for clarinets, even though Mozart doesn't exploit them to the degree that he would in Symphony No. 39. Indeed, there are few lengthy woodwind solos at all in this symphony; rather, Mozart treats his ensemble almost like a double choir, pitting the string section against the wind section, as in the dialogue that opens the first movement's second subject, or mixing string and wind timbres to produce gorgeous washes of color.

The first movement, with its absence of repeats, abundance of short motives, and festive pageantry, strikingly anticipates that of the "Posthorn" Serenade, composed a year later, except that, as befits a symphony, its material has more characterful thematic definition (and there is no slow introduction), which permits a more active development section. Indeed, the opening question-and-answer gesture (full orchestra followed by quiet strings) dominates the entire movement like a grand refrain, a persistent reminder of the source of the ensuing abundance of musical ideas of all shapes and sizes. Its prominence and habit of popping up at important junctures actually gives the movement something of a rondo character, even as it delineates the various sections of classical sonata form with singular clarity.

The central slow movement, like the first movement, contains a remarkable range of ideas of all shapes and sizes, and once again

I have to point to the lovely writing for woodwinds that colors its beautiful melodies, even though Mozart leaves out the trumpets, timpani, and clarinets. However, he saves the best for last. The racy finale goes like the wind, and features as its second subject a fugato that gives the whole wind section a moment in the sun, particularly as it gets expanded in the development section. This second subject tells us some very useful facts about Mozart's approach to symphonic form.

As I have already mentioned, a fugato is simply a melody repeated by one instrument after another, entering in sequence. If the music continues along these contrapuntal lines, it becomes a full-fledged fugue, but Mozart doesn't go any further than what would be considered the exposition of the fugue, hence the term *fugato* (which may be translated as "fuguelike"). In considering musical form back in chapter 1, I suggested that the effect of a fugue, particularly in instrumental music, is that of a discussion between the various participants. Nothing stops the narrative progression of incidents in a sonata movement more effectively than a lengthy pause for conversation.

Here Mozart's intention is to show off his musical prowess in a passage of dialogue at once witty and learned, which he deepens and expands in the development section. He is, in effect, offering the Parisian public a sort of musical resume (indeed, the whole symphony is that). In the recapitulation, however, Mozart wants to close in a blaze of brilliance and has no intention of stopping the action merely to honor some formal "rule," so he simply omits the fugato entirely so as to be able to wrap up the symphony with astonishing punctuality at high speed. Few other examples demonstrate so clearly the fact that in the hands of great composers, form always serves the music's expressive and dramatic needs—never the other way around.

Symphony No. 35 in D Major, K. 385 ("Haffner") (1782)

You might call this work "greatest hits from the second 'Haffner' Serenade," because Mozart put it together from a larger original that no longer exists. He added flutes and clarinets to the outer movements only to enrich the sound—they don't have important solos. In keeping with its serenade origins, the music is sunny and uncomplicated throughout. The first movement begins with a gesture so arresting that it dominates the entire movement, and it just so happens that you can sing the words "Here comes the Haffner!" to the opening five notes. You may also notice that the opening gesture and the quiet answer that follows it contain multiple repetitions of the Mozart rhythm.

When listening, try to pay special attention to what goes on below the music's surface, because the opening functions both as melody and as accompaniment, binding the entire exposition together by its omnipresence. It's particularly interesting to hear Mozart spread out the initial idea in successive statements by the various instruments, as though listeners are actually witnessing its growth and multiplication as the movement proceeds. The development section is also quite memorable, taking the main theme through darker minor keys with a feeling of weariness and resignation before the recapitulation restores the music's basic optimism.

The only word that adequately describes the slow movement is "adorable," although one might also consider "cuddly" or perhaps "kittenish." One of Mozart's great gifts as a melodist was his ability to write music that's sweet but never saccharine or kitschy, and here is a perfect example. A short and punchy minuet leads to a dazzling finale that Mozart directs should be played "as fast as possible." It's a bit silly to go into issues of form when the whole point of the music is speed: to whiz by and be finished before you can really think about it. This is light entertainment, classical style, at its very best.

Symphony No. 36 in C Major, K. 425 ("Linz") (1783)

In November of 1783, Mozart was passing through Linz on the way to Salzburg to introduce his new wife to his father, who was not at all happy about the marriage. During his stopover (and remember that in those days "stopovers" could last weeks), he was asked by a music-loving local aristocrat to give a concert and, in particular, to present a symphony. Having neglected to pack a few in his suitcase, Mozart wrote a new one—in four days. Perhaps it's this story, or perhaps it's the fact that Mozart only had oboes and bassoons handy for his woodwind section, but the "Linz" Symphony has never been as popular as the last three, or even the "Haffner," which is unaccountable because it's simply wonderful music all the way through.

I've already mentioned in the introduction to the symphonies how Mozart turned the small wind section to gorgeous advantage in the opening movement's second subject, which erupts in an angry minor key and continues with perhaps the sexiest chord ever written for soft oboes, bassoons, horns, and trumpets. In fact, the symphony's very opening, a stately adagio introduction, introduces the woodwinds with an important solo after only a few bars. The development section is also remarkably easy to follow: it's based entirely on the quiet little melodic tag that closes the exposition, so there's no mistaking exactly what is being developed.

The slow movement is also arresting in that it retains (for the first time in a major classical symphony) the full orchestra, including the trumpets and drums. Again, this may have been the result of the small wind section and Mozart's desire to keep the music as colorful as possible, but whatever the reason, the result has really impressive depth, especially when the music moves into minor keys. One can't help but get the impression that Mozart didn't write the music and "orchestrate" it, but rather conceived it entirely clothed and tailored to the intended instrumentation. Just try to imagine the music without those dramatic interjections of trumpets and timpani. It's impossible.

The minuet is very "Austrian" sounding, by which I mean it has a certain German dance (or "oompah") quality to its rhythms, particularly at the opening of the second half. Mozart gives listeners a finale in full sonata form. Once again the development section is especially clear. If you pay attention to the short outburst after the opening theme (it's the third loud interruption and the first by full orchestra, with trumpets and timpani), you will find that the development consists entirely of this little motive, chased throughout the orchestra, beginning with violins, then lower strings, then winds, alternating in various combinations. It may be that the music's very lucidity has counted against it among academics, but the really interesting fact is that the symphony's outer movements sound even more colorful than those of the "Haffner," which have the advantage (along with the "Paris" Symphony) of the largest symphonic orchestra that Mozart ever asked for. Go figure.

Symphony No. 38 in D Major, K. 504 ("Prague") (1786)

Symphony No. 37, as mentioned above, is actually by Michael Haydn, brother of Mozart's best friend Joseph and a notable Salzburg musician in his own right. Only its first movement introduction is by Mozart. It was originally included in the original complete edition of the symphonies, but since its true authorship has been determined, it has now gracefully retired from the scene.

Mozart composed No. 38 so as to have it ready during his trip to Prague for the first performances there in 1787 of *The Marriage of Figaro*. It was in the Czech capital, arguably to this day the most musical city in Europe, where Mozart first achieved popular success, and if he conceived this work as a sort of musical calling card, much like the "Paris" Symphony, then it speaks volumes of the taste and sophistication he expected of Czech music lovers. This is, arguably, at once the most intellectually intense (which is not to be confused with gratuitous complexity or obscurity) as well as the most physically exciting of the late symphonies, and the excitement stems entirely from the formal procedures that Mozart adopts.

Lest this sound daunting, I can sum up the facts very simply. The two outer movements continue their development sections right through the recapitulation of the first subjects, leaving it to the second subjects to reestablish the home key of D major. This practice produces incredible tension and forward momentum, especially since both development sections are extremely long and contrapuntally busy, bringing into combination all the important themes and motives from the expositions. This isn't a process about which you have to be fully conscious. After all, what you hear when listening is not so much the cause as the effect: in this case, an inexhaustible drive to the finish line propelled by large tracts of exhilarating orchestral activity. But let's take the music as it comes, in the order that Mozart wrote it, and all of this will become quite clear.

The "Prague" Symphony contains only three movements and, like the "Paris" Symphony, lacks a minuet. Some writers speculate that Mozart may have believed that Czech audiences preferred works in the old-fashioned Italian *sinfonia* style of fast–slow–fast. I find this a bit difficult to believe, given the fact that not only is Vienna much closer to Italy than Prague, but the work itself is fully half an hour long—that is, as long as or longer than any other Mozart symphony (including those with minuets), assuming equal treatment with respect to repeats. Furthermore, the absence of a dance movement somehow makes sense given the work's seriousness of content, even though it's not one of Mozart's minor-key works. In short, the music of the "Prague" Symphony strikes me as an attempt to enlarge the scale of the symphony as Mozart understood it and as he had used the medium up to that time.

The opening, an extremely broad and lengthy slow introduction, gives evidence of this new seriousness of purpose. It begins with a grand statement in jerky march rhythm answered by quiet sighs from the woodwinds. Clarinets truly being a Viennese specialty at this time, Mozart does not use them here. But in all other respects, the symphony pays eloquent tribute to the excellence of Czech wind players, a tradition still very much with us today. The introduction settles down to a flowing melody on the violins, but the mood soon darkens and a big minor-key section intervenes. This consists of dramatic chords for the full orchestra separated by rising sequences in the violins and leading ultimately to sorrowful phrases in the violins accompanied by a couple of creepy chromatic scales in the oboes and bassoons. The mood closely resembles the fearful introduction to the overture of *Don Giovanni* (an opera whose commission resulted from this trip and that was composed expressly for Prague).

The allegro opens with broad phrases in the lower strings over a syncopated rhythm in the first violins, immediately interrupted by the full wind section with trumpets and timpani. The scoring in this context can only be called garish, but there's a good reason for it, because the falling scale in the oboes and flutes that sounds etched in neon serves as a the basis for the entire development section, and Mozart wants you to remember it. Heard this way, it's practically impossible not to. A grand transition intervenes, leading to a broad restatement of the first subject without the wind interruption, and so on to the second subject scored at first for strings alone, first in the major and then immediately repeated in a haunting minor-key variant. The exposition closes with the motives of the first subject stated in different order— note in particular the phrase for low strings now repeated high in the violins.

After the exposition repeat, the development begins with the descending scale from the woodwind interruption of the open-ing theme. This becomes the backdrop for a vast development, in which Mozart basically works his way through everything heard so far in just about every conceivable combination. When the recapitulation arrives (with the descending scale in flutes and oboes now played quietly over the first theme without the assis-tance of the remaining winds, brass, and timpani), Mozart keeps right on developing, and by this I mean the home key refuses to establish itself with any feeling of security. That job falls to the second subject, an accomplishment that produces an overwhelm-ing feeling of relief as the music then pounds away at the home key to create a satisfying and extremely energetic close.

The slow movement begins with a broad phrase in the violins immediately interrupted by a long chromatic scale. The chro-maticism continues in various guises throughout the movement and has the characteristic effect of producing an incessant feeling of tonal instability. This is in fact a sonata movement without development section, full of extremely intricate detail for the wind section (absent trumpets and timpani). Mozart accom-plishes here through ornamentation the same ongoing feeling of development that he achieved in the first movement, only the result is an especially bewitching example of a continuously unfolding melody sometimes darkened by excursions into minor keys. Despite the very tightly controlled organization, the long lines and rhythmically free phrasing produce an effect of timeless spaciousness, almost of improvisation.

Although it lacks a slow introduction, the finale follows exactly the same formal pattern as the first movement, but in a sense that's not really the point. You may have a subconscious feeling for this sort of unity when thinking about the music in retrospect, but in real-time performance, what will strike you most forcefully is that the entire movement—first subject, second subject, development, and recapitulation—comes across as a vast, sustained dialogue between the strings and winds. Sometimes one section accompanies the other, but more often than not they oppose each other in sonic blocks, and the winds have long, unaccompanied passages all to themselves. This is Mozart's homage to the Czech wind tradition, and the exposition's closing theme (which also brings the symphony to a close), with its dancing flutes and oboes chiming like little bells above trilling strings, remains one of the most enchanting bits of orchestration of the classical period or any other.

The "Prague" Symphony provided Mozart with a way to enlarge the genre, not just formally, but also emotionally. All of his previous symphonies, with the exception of No. 25, were almost uniformly cheerful in tone. Mozart's remaining works in the form define the symphony as the most important genre of orchestral composition, not because of its formal intricacies, but because the sonata style permits an unprecedented depth and complexity of emotional expression through the medium of the orchestra alone. This was Mozart's great discovery, and this is the work in which he made it.

Symphony No. 39 in E-flat Major, K. 543 (1788)*
Symphony No. 40 in G Minor, K. 550 (1788)*
Symphony No. 41 in C Major, K. 551 ("Jupiter") (1788)*

These three symphonies, Mozart's last, deserve to be treated together, since although we do not know for what occasion they were composed or when they were performed, they stand as a set and contrast so very nicely with each other. For example, No. 39 has clarinets instead of oboes, No. 40 has both (in its revised version), and No. 41 has oboes only. Only No. 39 has a slow introduction, only No. 40 is written in a minor key, and only No. 41 makes such extensive use of counterpoint in its finale. I could go on, but I'm sure that you get the picture.

On the other hand, there is a very real sense in which these works build on the enlargement of Mozart's emotional range as a symphonist as encountered in the "Prague" Symphony, and for that reason they can correctly be heard as extensions of that work. For example, Symphony No. 39 continues Mozart's exploration of the possibilities of a long, slow introduction to the first movement. In No. 40, Mozart turns the "Prague" Symphony's richer emotional depth loose on a work based in a minor key with devastating results, while the "Jupiter" Symphony (dumb nickname, by the way, and not Mozart's) might be said in its finale to carry the ongoing developmental process in the outer movements of the "Prague" to their logical conclusion.

I want to briefly touch on the various aspects of each work that make it particularly distinctive, with the understanding that my general remarks regarding Symphony No. 38 apply equally here and so do not need to be repeated. The emotional riches contained in these pieces can only be suggested verbally; it's up

---

* See also "What Makes Mozart Sound Like Mozart?"

to each listener to live with the music and gradually arrive at a personal understanding of what it means and expresses.

Symphony No. 39 in E-flat Major

This is the least familiar of the three symphonies, which is odd because it's also the most purely euphonious and cheerful. The slow introduction, which opens with the Mozart rhythm, is note-worthy for the broad contrasts between grand proclamations for full orchestra and downward-sweeping violin scales. Remember these scales, because they reappear in the transition from first subject to second subject once the allegro gets underway, and so weld the introduction to the body of the movement in the most graphic possible way.

Both the first and second subjects employ odd phrase lengths and offbeat accents to create the delightful sense of something slightly off kilter—like a debutante at her first ball who hasn't quite learned how to waltz. This generates a lot of rhythmic tension even though the basic dynamic for both subjects remains very quiet, and it contrasts in the strongest possible way with rhythmically regular transitional material. Even though, as I said, the basic mood is cheerful, the music is full of half-tints and harmonic shadings characteristic of Mozart's newly acquired sense of depth, and enriched by the velvety tone of the two clarinets.

Indeed, one of the things that the symphony is definitely "about" is the timbre of those two woodwind instruments. They make their presence felt everywhere but particularly in their radiant contributions to the slow movement, and in the trio of the sturdy-sounding minuet, where the tune and accompaniment they have wouldn't sound out of place on a carnival merry-go-round. The finale, on the other hand, depends less on characterful themes than it does on its first seven notes, which generate both the first and second subjects. If you can count to seven in really fast tempo, you will find endless delight in Mozart's play with this opening motive. Just how this music enlarges his compositional range is a subjective question. My own opinion is this: we often see the words "witty" and "cheerful" used to describe Mozart's major-key music, but the delicious woodwind interjections that interrupt that ubiquitous seven-note roulade when it appears as the second subject can only be called "droll."

Symphony No. 40 in G Minor

Even people who have never heard of Mozart know the opening theme of this symphony, and not just because it seems to have been programmed into the ring signal of so many cellular telephones (a principal source of classical music in the modern age). It remains the apotheosis of Mozartean pathos, music that perhaps can best be described as expressing grace under fearful pressure. The comparative coolness of the slow movement makes it an island of calm and relaxation in what otherwise would be a uniformly tense listening experience. Contrast this with Mozart's very different procedure (that of providing a "happy" finale) in the otherwise even more anguished G Minor String Quintet.

An interesting parallel between these two great G minor works concerns their minuets, in both of which the music's despairing harshness contrasts very sharply with its ostensibly dancelike qualities. Indeed in the symphony, the combination of a minor key harnessed to tightly woven form is so effective in conveying a sense of tragic inevitability that it inspired Mozart to write one of classical music's first genuinely angry finales, an object he accomplished by the simple expedient of applying a particularly symmetrical sonata formula. This tension between the expressive violence of the themes and the ruthless logic of their presentation generates much of the music's implacable power.

Only one further point needs to be made regarding this symphony. Mozart originally composed it for oboes without clarinets, but he later rewrote the oboe parts to permit the addition of his most beloved woodwind instruments. Controversy has raged ever since over which version is better. Proponents of the revised version point out that using clarinets reflects Mozart's clear preference. This is indisputable. On the other hand, some listeners and conductors feel that the nasal, cutting tone of the oboes accentuates the gaunt, grim qualities of the music in a way that the softer timbre of clarinets can only compromise. I invite you to listen and draw your own conclusions. The recording included on the accompanying CD uses the revised version, and the easiest way to hear the difference in the complete work is to check the end of the minuet, where the oboes (or clarinets) have a prominent solo.

Symphony No. 41 in C Major, K. 551 ("Jupiter")

The unfortunate nickname was the inspiration of Johann Peter Salomon, the savvy London impresario responsible for Haydn's successes there. It was in London that a deeply shocked Haydn learned of Mozart's death (he never fully got over it) and raved about his friend's accomplishments to English musical society. Salomon would have dearly loved to add Mozart to his roster of attractions. I have no idea what a Roman god sounds like, but I think I'm on pretty firm ground when I say that he probably does not sound like Mozart's Symphony No. 41. On the other hand, the title does come in handy and sounds better than a bald numerical designation, so we're stuck with it.

Perhaps the most purely beautiful moment in this grand and festive symphony occurs in the sublime (there's no other word for it) slow movement, when it veers into a minor key, and palpitating violins accompany long, arching phrases in the solo woodwinds. The effect is breathtaking, and a contrast made all the stronger by the fact that most of the other themes in the symphony consist of tags and formulas, the common coin of the Viennese classical style. Mozart points this out when he uses the witty theme from "Un bacio di mano" (CD track 7) as part of the first movement's second subject (CD track 1 at 2:33), after a dramatic minor-key outburst (recall the one at the same place in the "Linz" Symphony). Once again the impression is very droll: a comic "tune" with the chutzpah to appear amidst the first move-ment's very proper and serious trumpeting and drumming. It's sort of the musical equivalent of that wonderful scene in the film *This Is Spinal Tap* when the hard rock band gets booked to appear at a very conservative "mixer" on a military base.

The finale of the "Jupiter" Symphony is justly celebrated as a contrapuntal tour-de-force and perhaps the greatest example of Mozart's mosaic technique: building a big movement up from little motives or musical formulas. Unfortunately, while most people will celebrate the music's polyphonic mastery, very few will tell you what it means in terms of what you actually hear. However, I think we know enough about sonata form to under-stand what Mozart accomplishes and how this movement once again enlarges the possibilities of what symphonic music can be.

As noted in the discussion of the fugato second subject of the finale of the "Paris" Symphony, an extended passage of formal counterpoint has the effect of a musical conversation: its effect is rhetorical rather than dramatic. This is why actual fugues (as opposed to the use of melodic counterpoint in general) are com-paratively rare within sonata movements, although they may occur as independent pieces in the context of larger works. The effect of a fugue in the middle of a sonata movement is rather like that of a watching a scene from a play or movie and then listening to a bunch of critics or commentators discuss what they have just seen. It stops the progress of the drama dead in its tracks.

There will always be moments when this sort of change of focus is exactly the right thing in the right place; the amount of counterpoint is essentially a function of what expressive point the composer wishes to make. Mozart's finale, on the other hand, while not a formal fugue, is both contrapuntal *throughout* and a perfect example of full sonata form *throughout*. Aside from some transitional material, there are no extended themes at all, just combinations of a few clear and catchy motives. The effect of this fusion of genres is remarkable, akin to a drama whose subject is an ongoing conversation between a definite number of characters. There are five basic motives (not counting connecting tissue and accompaniment figures), the first of which is the famous opening with its four long notes.

There is precedent for this type of construction in the arts: think of the play (and movie) *12 Angry Men,* which concerns a jury deliberation. Is the play any less interesting, less passion- ate, or less impressive because of its special structure, or do the circumstances of its premise make it a uniquely powerful state- ment in which the dramatic tension arises from group dynamics and progress of the debate? Translate this concept into music and you have Mozart's finale—a fitting if sadly premature end to his symphonic legacy.

Opera Overtures

Der Schauspieldirektor, K. 486 (1786)
The Marriage of Figaro, K. 492 (1786)
Don Giovanni, K. 527 (1787)*
Così fan tutte, K. 588 (1790)
The Magic Flute, K. 620 (1791)

N o Mozart collection is complete without a selection of
his opera overtures. Needless to say, it's worthwhile
to have the complete operas too, but these movements work perfectly well independently and constitute some
of Mozart's most colorful and entertaining music. Besides,
believe it or not, some people don't even *like* opera, whether
Mozart's or anyone else's, but do love terrific orchestral music.
Some of these overtures, such as the last three listed above,
quote themes from the operas they introduce, while the
others suggest their emotional ambience and leave it at that.
Both *Der Schauspieldirektor* (The Impresario) and *The Marriage of
Figaro* are essays in comic hysteria, frenzied music that trips over
itself in an excess of exaggerated high spirits. *Don Giovanni* (CD
track 11), as already has been seen, contains the most frighten-
ing music that Mozart ever wrote and constitutes a milestone in
musical history as one of the first attempts to describe supernatural terror in pure sound. The remainder of the overture is light-
hearted comedy. *Così fan tutte* can only be described as "gossipy."
Wind instruments take turns passing a sly little theme off to

---

* See also "What Makes Mozart Sound Like Mozart?"

each other while the orchestra interjects with exclamations of delight. Finally, *The Magic Flute* mingles music of great solemnity and serenity with one of Mozart's most madcap allegros. These are the highlights: there are quite a few more overtures than these, and most recordings will contain several others that you can explore at your leisure.

Part 4

Concertos

Introduction

M ozart was unarguably the greatest concerto writer that ever lived, and so this is necessarily the largest group of pieces up for consideration. However, discussion in detail of twenty-one individual works all in the same genre would defeat the purpose of a practical guide for listening and suggest something along the lines of an encyclopedia, not to mention the fact that I would necessarily spend a great deal of time (more than I have already) repeatedly mentioning common formal elements, while perhaps giving too much significance to technical minutiae in attempting to differentiate one work from the next. This problem applies particularly to the piano concertos, less so to the other works.

In any event, a different approach seems called for than with the other orchestral works, so first I'll discuss Mozart's invention of a special kind of sonata form for his concerto first movements. Mozart really perfected this particular method of organization, and in doing so, he basically annihilated the work of his contemporaries to the degree that, historically speaking, there are no concertos for any instrument by any other composer in the second half the eighteenth century (aside from a couple by Haydn for instruments—trumpet and cello—not covered by Mozart) that most listeners care about today. Then, once I've covered the formal aspect, I will use that as the framework for a brief consideration of the individual works in small groups, focusing on useful comparisons, expressive similarities, and helpful means of entry into what might otherwise seem a dauntingly large body of work. This music took over a decade and a half of Mozart's short life to compose and so deserves to be savored.

Mozart's Concerto Form

It's easy to understand why Mozart was such a fantastic composer of concertos, since the requirements are exactly those that make a great composer of vocal music: a mastery of the long, singing line and the ability to organize the interaction between the soloist (or singer) and orchestra in terms of the melodies allocated and shared between them. This is all that *concerto form* in the classical period really is, and Mozart's use of it is always designed to focus and enrich each work's emotional vocabulary.

Essentially the only movement that distinguishes concertos from other kinds of orchestral works is the first, because it employs sonata form. Rondos, variations, and slow movements of various types, where the music is either predominantly lyrical or naturally falls into a series of self-sufficient sections, lend themselves well to the alternation between solo and orchestra and invariably benefit from the built-in opportunities for contrast that the concerto offers. Sonata-form movements present a special problem that needs solving, since the presence of the soloist needs to be "explained" and integrated into the musical narrative. In other words, the soloist has to work with the orchestra, not just play off it, dominate it, or be dominated by it. The basic issue can be accurately defined as the need to write a movement describing the actions of two independent characters (soloist and orchestra) rather than one (orchestra alone).

Happily, sonata form has a mechanism perfectly designed to help the resourceful composer achieve this goal, assuming that composer recognizes its usefulness in the first place (and this is where Mozart differs from most of his contemporaries and successors). We are already very familiar with this mechanism: the exposition repeat. In a purely orchestral work, this device is generally a literal return to the beginning of the exposition, and it may or may not be observed by the performers. In a concerto, Mozart allocates the first statement of the exposition to the orchestra alone, where it has the effect of an introduction, and the repeat introduces the soloist who may also (and usually does) have his or her own additional themes to add.

The possibilities inherent in this procedure are truly immense. Remember that there are no rules as to which tunes or motives can go into a sonata form's first or second subject. Add to this fact Mozart's realization that the first exposition should not leave the home key for any length of time because this begins the process of development without the soloist. So he reserves until the second exposition the first important move away from home, and this means that only the participation of the soloist permits listeners to hear the two definitive subjects in their proper keys, with all of the various themes and motives (including any new ones introduced by the solo) allocated between them. This in turn produces even more opportunities for fun in the recapitulation, which is only heard once and which has to take into account (or not) all the material from *both* expositions.

From this explanation, I think it's pretty clear that Mozart, with his love of writing on a large scale, developed this concept of first-movement concerto form not because it was especially complicated but because it gave him an almost limitless number of choices as to how to create, arrange, and develop his musical ideas, and it required a good bit of space (that is, time) in which to do it. Many of Mozart's concerto first movements are nearly as long as the remainder of the work, and although his concertos have three instead of four movements (because of this extra length), even the early ones almost invariably outlast any of the contemporary symphonies. Finally, consider also that Mozart was one of the greatest pianists of his day and that most of these works were composed for his own use. Given these facts, his special relationship with the concerto (especially for piano) should be quite understandable.

Only one additional matter remains to be explained. Because the entire point of the first exposition is to prepare for the entry of the soloist and to establish the orchestra as an equal partner in the proceedings, at the very end of the movement, the orchestra will always pause and let the soloist have his or her own say in the form of a *cadenza*, theoretically, an improvisation based on the themes of the concerto. The cadenza gives the soloist a chance to show off, to display his or her taste and musicianship, and to counterbalance that long orchestral introduction. Real improvisation in performance today is rare. Mozart wrote down some of his own cadenzas, and soloists today will either use them, use someone else's (such as Beethoven's for Piano Concerto No. 20), or compose their own according to their particular artistic inclinations.

Concertos for Strings

Violin Concerto No. 3 in G Major, K. 216 (1775)
Violin Concerto No. 5 in A Major, K. 219 (1775)*
Sinfonia Concertante for Violin and Viola in E-flat
  Major, K. 364 (1779)

At the age of nineteen, Mozart wrote five violin concertos that represent his only essays in the form. As a rule, and even at this early stage in the development of the modern orchestra, violin concertos are terribly difficult to get right. The problems of balance—even with the small ensemble here consisting only of strings, two oboes (or flutes), and two horns—make the composer's job a tough one, and it's no mystery why later composers of famous works in the genre, such as Beethoven, Brahms, Tchaikovsky, Dvořák, and Sibelius, only wrote a single work apiece.

That said, Mozart's last three essays in this challenging genre are the only violin concertos in the international repertoire that fall chronologically between those of baroque masters, such as Bach and Vivaldi, and Beethoven's great concerto from the first decade of the nineteenth century. While not exactly "mature" Mozart, they have great charm and an abundance of good tunes. I include Concerto No. 3 because of its heavenly slow movement, a stunning example of Mozart's early vocal style. Flutes take over from oboes in assisting the soloist with an unforgettable melody that clearly served as model for Mozart's most famous "singing" andante, the great slow movement of Piano Concerto No. 21.

* See also"What Makes Mozart Sound Like Mozart?"

Violin Concerto No. 5 has a nickname, the "Turkish," which comes from the dashing minor-key episode in its rondo finale. As discussed in "What Makes Mozart Sound Like Mozart," this movement serves as a particularly clear exemplar of the form in a concerto context, with a ritornello in the shape of a gracious minuet and highly contrasted episodes. The entire work is certainly worth hearing, as is the Fourth Concerto, and recordings of the entire set are readily available.

One possible reason that Mozart didn't continue writing violin concertos (aside from the fact that no one paid him to write more, which may be the best reason of all) could be what he perceived as the limitations of opposing a single stringed instrument to the full orchestra. His greatest string concerto in fact has two soloists, which is all that "sinfonia concertante" means in this context—more than one soloist. Mozart preferred the viola above all other strings, and he probably played the solo part himself. The addition of another soloist means that everything important will be said at least three times: by the orchestra as well as by each string player in turn, and that gives Mozart ample opportunity to do what he does best—expand his form by writing gorgeous tunes.

This is, accordingly, a large work. It plays for a good half an hour, and the slow movement is nearly as long as the very ample first movement—as well as being set in a minor key and containing some of Mozart's most poignantly expressive sad music. The only reason you don't hear this piece more often is because of the logistical difficulty of getting together two first-class soloists, for this is in every other respect great Mozart and certainly the finest double concerto for stringed instruments before Brahms's famous example written over a hundred years later (for violin and cello). If you only have room in your collection for a single Mozart string concerto, then this is it.

Concertos for Winds

Flute Concerto No. 1 in G Major, K. 313 (1778)
Flute Concerto No. 2 in D Major, K. 314 (1778)
Clarinet Concerto in A Major, K. 622 (1791)

The two flute concertos may not be Mozart at his most mature, but like the early violin concertos they are delightful pieces, and more to the point they are the only important flute concertos in existence by a universally acknowledged great composer, out of what seem like zillions, written between the baroque period and the twentieth century. That means the flutists play them constantly (as well as the Concerto for Flute and Harp), probably more than they deserve, but that's another issue. Mozart allegedly detested the flute as a solo instrument, which isn't a bit surprising considering that it's far more limited technically speaking than the violin, but since he was constitutionally incapable of not solving a musical problem once he got his hands on it, he produced this pair of classics that not only showcases the flute but manages to be (especially in the slow movements) pretty fine Mozart as well.

The Clarinet Concerto is another story. There are in the repertoire, among a number of lesser essays in the genre, basically two large-scale, truly major works for this instrument: this one, and the concerto by twentieth-century Danish composer Carl Nielsen. Given Mozart's love of the instrument and the late date of composition (just before his death), listeners have every right to expect a great work, and that's what he delivers. Perhaps the most interesting thing about the piece sonically speaking is that the orchestra includes no oboes or clarinets, making the soloist the only mid-range wind instrument. This has the subtle effect of creating a sort of "bracket" between the flutes and bassoons, throwing a gentle spotlight on the soloist. The tunes in all three movements are also especially attractive, and supremely vocal in inspiration. A top-notch soloist in this work really can create the illusion that one is in fact listening to a singer as much as to an instrumentalist.

Piano Concertos

As with the symphonies, and for the same reason, I provide below a little chart showing the orchestration of each of the piano concertos under consideration. You can learn more about what to listen for in any work of Mozart just by knowing who's playing than by almost any amount of verbal explanation, because you can almost always be sure that the music will take full advantage of the resources employed. Aside from being one of the great keyboard virtuosos of his age, Mozart's great advantage in writing piano concertos is that this particular instrument, along with its extended dynamic range, can make a complete mass of harmony all by itself and thus truly challenge the orchestra on its own terms. That is basically what all these concertos are: an interactive, dramatic narrative involving two equal characters.

However, as I mentioned above, I am not going to go into lengthy descriptions of each of these fifteen concertos. Rather, I am going to take the variety and subtlety of Mozart's first-movement form for granted, and instead group the various works so as to suggest what I hope will strike you as useful and interesting listening comparisons. You can then use these to select, according to your personal taste and inclinations, your own means of entry into this extraordinarily rich musical world.

Concerto No.	Instruments in Addition to Strings and Piano						
	flutes	oboes	clarinets	bassoons	horns	trumpets	timpani (pairs)
9		2			2		
14		2			2		
15		2		2	2		
16	1	2		2	2	2	1
17	1	2		2	2		
18	1	2		2	2		
19	1	2		2	2		
20	1	2		2	2	2	1
21	1	2		2	2	2	1
22	1		2	2	2	2	1
23	1		2	2	2		
24	1	2	2	2	2	2	1
25	1	2		2	2	2	1
26	1	2		2	2	2	1
27	1	2		2	2		

Group 1: 1784—The Watershed Year

Piano Concerto No. 14 in E-flat Major, K. 449 (1784)
Piano Concerto No. 15 in B-flat Major, K. 450 (1784)
Piano Concerto No. 16 in D Major, K. 451 (1784)
Piano Concerto No. 17 in G Major, K. 453 (1784)*
Piano Concerto No. 18 in B-flat Major, K. 456 (1784)
Piano Concerto No. 19 in F Major, K. 459 (1784)

It's probably fair to say that Mozart never matched the sheer variety and sustained musical quality of the six piano concertos that he wrote in 1784. The orchestration in the first three is particularly interesting. No. 14 only asks for oboes and horns in addition to the strings, and it is written so that they can be omitted entirely and the work actually performed at home with

---

* See also "What Makes Mozart Sound Like Mozart?"

a solo string quintet. On the other hand, No. 15 throws down the orchestral gauntlet, actually beginning with a woodwind solo, while No. 16 adds trumpets and timpani. If this first great flowering of the classical piano concerto as a genre interests you particularly, then this is the place to start.

Group 2: Soulful Slow Movements

Piano Concerto No. 9 in E-flat Major, K. 271 (1777)
Piano Concerto No. 18 in B-flat Major, K. 456 (1784)
Piano Concerto No. 23 in A Major, K. 488 (1786)

These three concertos all feature slow movements in minor keys, and that always means the expression of pathos, sadness, and melancholy. Concerto No. 9 also has the distinction of being Mozart's first great concerto, and it had the best possible inspiration: a woman. Her name was Mlle. Jeunehomme, and the concerto itself is sometimes known as the "Jeunehomme" Concerto for that reason. The opening of this concerto is special in that its initial question-and-answer theme features the orchestra and piano in turn right off the bat, before the orchestra then proceeds with its long opening exposition. This has the effect of Mozart saying: "Here are two equal partners. Now watch me prove it."

Piano Concertos No. 18 and 23 are also special in other ways. No. 18's slow movement is a theme and variations, the only one in this position in any of the piano concertos. No. 23, on the other hand, omits oboes entirely in favor of clarinets, just like Symphony No. 39, composed two years later. So in addition to having slow movements of particular expressiveness on the sad side of the emotional spectrum, each of these works shows Mozart exploring new formal and orchestral possibilities.

Group 3: Themes and Variations

Piano Concerto No. 17 in G Major, K. 453 (1784)*
Piano Concerto No. 18 in B-flat Major, K. 456 (1784)
Piano Concerto No. 24 in C Minor, K. 491 (1786)

These are the three concertos that include variation movements. Interestingly two of them are in minor keys (K. 456 and K. 491), while two of them are finales (K. 453 and K. 491). As I just mentioned, K. 456's example is a central slow movement. Since I discuss the finale of Concerto No. 17 very thoroughly in "What Makes Mozart Sound Like Mozart?" and it's included on your accompanying CD (track 4), if you enjoy following Mozart's imagination as he puts a simple tune through its paces, you may well want to consider these.

Group 4: Fun with Counterpoint

Piano Concerto No. 14 in E-flat Major, K. 449 (1784)
Piano Concerto No. 19 in F Major, K. 459 (1784)

Both of these concertos have finales that integrate contrapuntal episodes within sonata-rondo form. In the discussion of the finale of the "Jupiter" Symphony, I noted how counterpoint can be problematic in a sonata-form first movement, as it substitutes discussion for dramatic action, but in finales this may very well be just the ticket, since conversation relaxes the level of tension and offers additional opportunities for wit. Both of these concertos take advantage of this fact, but in very different ways. The ritornello theme of Concerto No. 14's rondo is a perky phrase that always appears in counterpoint as it gets tossed between the

---

* See also "What Makes Mozart Sound Like Mozart?"

soloist and the strings. Concerto No. 19's finale, on the other hand, opens with a rondo theme alternating piano and winds, and it's the strings that have a tendency to interrupt with lengthy debates about what they have just heard. Their seriousness contrasts delightfully with the comic tone of the opening tune.

Group 5: What a Month!

Piano Concerto No. 20 in D Minor, K. 466 (1785)
Piano Concerto No. 21 in C Major, K. 467 (1785)*

These two concertos, possibly Mozart's most popular and best known, are polar opposites. No. 20 inhabits the same stormy world as the opening of the overture to *Don Giovanni,* while No. 21 (the horribly named "Elivra Madigan" Concerto, after a Swedish film that almost no one has ever seen) contains Mozart's most dreamy and romantic slow movement. Both were composed within the space of a month in 1785. Listen and be amazed.

Group 6: Happy Hunting

Piano Concerto No. 15 in B-flat Major, K. 450 (1784)
Piano Concerto No. 22 in E-flat Major, K. 482 (1785)

You have already seen several examples of the hunting style in Mozart's chamber music and symphonies. The concertos also take part in this festive activity, most famously in the case of the four horn concertos, which were "born to hunt," more or less. But these two concertos also enjoy a final romp through the royal game park, led by two remarkably similar opening tunes.

---

* See also "What Makes Mozart Sound Like Mozart?"

Group 7: Clarinets

Piano Concerto No. 22 in E-flat Major, K. 482 (1785)
Piano Concerto No. 23 in A Major, K. 488 (1786)
Piano Concerto No. 24 in C Minor, K. 491 (1786)

These are the three concertos that have clarinets in their wood-wind sections (in Nos. 22 and 23 instead of oboes, in No. 24 in addition to them). Indeed, No. 22 contains the most lavish wind writing of any Mozart concerto, so much so that the wind section almost becomes a third participant in addition to the piano and the full orchestra. In No. 24, the clarinets add color to this intense and often anguished work, because as you can hear for yourself, nothing in the orchestra wails quite like a woodwind section in full cry.

Group 8: Minor Keys

Piano Concerto No. 20 in D Minor, K. 466 (1785)
Piano Concerto No. 24 in C Minor, K. 491 (1786)

As with the symphonies, there are only two Mozart concertos based in minor keys, but both are two of his greatest works in any medium. Because Mozart's minor-key works are so immediately communicative (of sadness, granted) and so universally admired, you may want to start with these and then gradually take on the happier works. Notice that I said "happier" and not "lighter." One of the more interesting points of comparison between these two pieces is the fact that No. 20 manages a comic ending, while No. 24 stays grimly in the minor right up to its last chord.

Group 9: Military Concertos

Piano Concerto No. 16 in D Major, K. 451 (1784)
Piano Concerto No. 21 in C Major, K. 467 (1785)*
Piano Concerto No. 25 in C Major, K. 503 (1786)
Piano Concerto No. 26 in D Major, K. 537 ("Coronation")
  (1788)

We can never quite recapture, with the sound of the massive modern orchestra in our ears, the thrill of trumpets and drums as instruments of war. It is worth remembering that when Mozart needed trumpeters, he often turned to musicians employed by the local militia, and kettledrums were found not in a musical instrument storage room but in the local armory. Far from being the giant copper tubs that we see today, timpani in Mozart's day were small and designed to be hung over the back of a horse and played while in the saddle (although not, we presume, when used at a concert).

The "military" concerto, with trumpets and drums and a first movement in moderate march tempo, is a mini-genre all by itself. Perhaps the most famous example is Beethoven's "Emperor" Concerto, and it will come as a surprise to some that Mozart's Concerto No. 21, best known for its glorious slow movement, is probably the most military of them all everywhere else. This of course makes that slow movement even more special when heard as it should be, in its proper context sandwiched between two energetic, trumpet- and timpani-laden partners.

---

* See also "What Makes Mozart Sound Like Mozart?"

Group 10: Chamber Concertos

Piano Concerto No. 19 in F Major, K. 459 (1784)
Piano Concerto No. 23 in A Major, K. 488 (1786)
Piano Concerto No. 27 in B-flat Major, K. 595 (1791)

At the opposite end from the grand, festive military concertos and the anguished minor-key works lies a very special subclassification, as much a matter of subjective impression as of musical procedure. By *chamber concerto* I do not mean a work such as Concerto No. 14, which can be played as an actual chamber piece by leaving out the wind parts and using solo strings. Rather, it means a concerto that downplays flashy solo display in favor of dialogue between the soloist and the orchestra, with numerous intimate exchanges among the piano and the various musicians (especially the winds).

The above works seem to fit this category especially well. Certainly the last piano concerto of all, No. 27, has a chamber-music quality in its gently soulful dialogue with the orchestra. However, all three of these wonderful pieces feature smallish orchestras (that is, without trumpets and timpani, and with either oboes or clarinets but never both) that Mozart uses with maximum resourcefulness and refinement in creating every possible kind of interaction with the piano. Certainly they are no less expressive for being subtle, and attentive listeners may well find their emotional world even more accessible than that projected by the larger, grander, more public concertos.

Conclusion
Strategies for Listening

Mozart makes great background music and terrific light entertainment. There's also no one better for those intimate, "quiet listening" moments. I say this not to be cynical but because it's the truth and a perfectly legitimate use of his music. Indeed, it's the reason that Mozart wrote a good part of it in the first place, as we have seen. The works selected for discussion in this book differ from this paradigm only to the extent that they also repay repetition and as much attention as you can comfortably give them. In today's world, with such a vast amount of entertainment on offer in so many genres, there's only so much leisure time in a day, and there's no getting around the fact that listening to music in large forms will use up as much of that time as you have to spare.

The point I want to make here, however, is that it's not a question of either treating the music purely as background to some other activity or planting yourself in a chair and gazing into space as the music washes over you. There's room for both approaches, certainly, but also for every gradation in between, and the trick for everyone, even us music "professionals," lies in finding the best use of the time we have and determining what place each type of listening experience warrants in our busy lives given our love of music in general. Getting the *most* out of Mozart will therefore necessarily depend on how much time you want to spend, but you will get *something* out of Mozart no matter what that amount is.

With this in mind, I have put together the following five groups consisting of selected pieces I have covered throughout this book. A couple of these lists build on the categories I proposed for listening to the piano concertos, here expanded to take into account the entire range of genres under discussion. You can use any of them as a convenient basis around which to organize your Mozart listening sessions. I then offer for your consideration and amusement my own personal "Top 10," which I hope you can use as a springboard in coming up with your own equally enlightened choices.

I. Themes and Variations

Divertimento in E flat, K. 563, for string trio
String Quartet No. 15 in D Minor, K. 421
String Quartet No. 18 in A Major, K. 464
Clarinet Quintet in A Major, K. 581
String Quintet in E-flat Major, K. 614
Wind Serenade No. 10 in B-flat Major, K. 361 ("Gran Partita")
Wind Serenade No. 12 in C Minor, K. 388
Piano Concerto No. 17 in G Major, K. 453
Piano Concerto No. 18 in B-flat Major, K. 456
Piano Concerto No. 24 in C Minor, K. 491

All musical form relies on three basic qualities: repetition, variation, and your own memory. When you listen to a sonata-form development or recapitulation, you are hearing the art of variation. The second exposition in a concerto first movement is another type, as is the return of the ritornello in a rondo. For this reason, movements in strict variation form offer an ideal opportunity to enjoyably get a handle on what composers do with tunes both there and in the context of other, less sectional forms.

When listening to a set of variations, the most important point to keep in mind is that the theme has many components, any one of which may be developed (or ignored), including melody, harmony, rhythm, tonality, accompaniment, phrase length, ornamentation, or any other audible fact that seizes a composer's imagination. The majority of Mozart's variation movements are keyboard solos, but some of his most imaginative and colorful examples of this form went into his great chamber and orchestral works, including these.

2. The Hunt

String Quartet No. 17 in B-flat Major, K. 458
String Quintet in E-flat Major, K. 614
Symphony No. 29 in A Major, K. 201
Piano Concerto No. 15 in B-flat Major, K. 450
Piano Concerto No. 22 in E-flat Major, K. 482

It's difficult today to imagine the importance of this social activity in the eighteenth century, particularly among the aristocracy, but it rivaled the march and the dance as a subject for musical stylization, and all composers of the period paid it homage, nowhere more so than in the galloping first movement of Beethoven's Seventh Symphony. As I mentioned in talking about the two piano concertos with hunting finales, Mozart's most famous movements in this style not surprisingly come from his four horn concertos (the horn being the hunting instrument of choice, just as trumpets and timpani are the military instruments of choice).

Interestingly, the hunt movements in the two chamber works listed above are not finales but opening movements, which is quite unusual because the quick 6/8 meter typical of this kind of music often signals a composer's intention to avoid the rigors of sonata form and write a carefree, less highly organized piece. What Mozart achieves here (one of his legacies from Haydn) is a carefree, very highly organized movement indeed, and that makes his achievement all the greater.

3. The Great Minor-Key Works

Piano Quartet in G Minor, K. 478
String Quartet No. 15 in D Minor, K. 421
String Quintet in G Minor, K. 516
Wind Serenade No. 12 in C Minor, K. 388
Piano Concerto No. 20 in D Minor, K. 466
Piano Concerto No. 24 in C Minor, K. 491
Symphony No. 25 in G Minor, K. 183
Symphony No. 40 in G Minor, K. 550

I'm always of two minds about grouping works by their emotional qualities, particularly when this can give substance to the lie that the only "deep" feelings are sad or depressing ones, and that greatness is a function of the degree to which an artist expresses suffering. Mozart is such a multidimensional composer in any case that even a work as "light" as *Eine Kleine Nachtmusik* takes more than passing notice of the expressive value of minor keys, and I've also discussed how the G Minor String Quintet, perhaps the saddest music in all of Mozart, concludes with one of his happiest finales. We must never forget that what matters in this music is emotional range and variety, and not recourse to extremes.

On the other hand, what makes these works so special is Mozart's almost invariable habit of remaining in the minor key in sonata-form recapitulations, whereas most other composers would switch to the tonic major so as to provide a happy ending. There's something very satisfying in hearing emotional intensity arising directly from a uniquely rigorous view of form. When all is said and done, there's no better proof of the fact that in Mozart, form and content—what he wants to express and the way he expresses it—are perfectly wed.

4. Celebrations and Calling Cards

"Haffner" Serenade in D Major, K. 250
"Posthorn" Serenade in D Major, K. 320
Symphony No. 31 in D Major, K. 297 ("Paris")
Symphony No. 35 in D Major, K. 385 ("Haffner")
Symphony No. 36 in C Major, K. 425 ("Linz")
Symphony No. 38 in D Major, K. 504 ("Prague")

Here are some of the works that Mozart wrote for large public festivities or used to establish himself in the great musical capitals of Europe. All of them are celebratory scores with trumpets and timpani, full of energy, contrast, and variety. You can almost see Mozart at his writing table working on the eighth movement of the "Haffner" Serenade, saying: "This is gonna slay 'em!" And so it did, at least to the extent that he was asked to compose another one, which survives as the "Haffner" Symphony.

The two most important pieces in this group strike me as the "Posthorn" Serenade, perhaps the most purely colorful and varied orchestral work that Mozart ever wrote, and the "Prague" Symphony, in which the symphony "grows up," transforming itself before listeners' eyes and ears from a bubbly curtain raiser or warm-up act preceding the musical main attraction to a genuine event whose depth and range of expression carries the genre to the forefront of the world of instrumental music.

5. Enlarging the Medium

Divertimento in E flat, K. 563, for string trio
Piano and Wind Quintet in E-flat Major, K. 452
String Quintet in C Major, K. 515
Wind Serenade No. 10 in B-flat Major, K. 361 ("Gran Partita")
"Haffner" Serenade in D Major, K. 250
Sinfonia Concertante for Violin and Viola in E-flat Major, K. 364
Piano Concerto No. 9 in E-flat Major, K. 271
Symphony No. 38 in D Major, K. 504 ("Prague")

You might call this selection "Ultimate Mozart," for it reveals him at his biggest, boldest, most expansive, and often most creative. Many of these works, such as the "Gran Partita," Divertimento for string trio, and "Haffner" Serenade remain the largest works ever composed in their respective genres. The others all represent milestones in the history of their media. The Quintet for Piano and Winds took the language of sonata form and made glorious music out of what appears to be a hopelessly clumsy and dysfunctional assortment of instruments.

Mozart's String Quintet in C contains his largest-ever opening movement and essentially defines a "quintet style" as distinct from that of the string quartets. Piano Concerto No. 9 is widely considered his first truly great work in any form, and it's also the first great classical piano concerto in Western history, while the Sinfonia Concertante is the largest and most powerful string concerto before Beethoven's Violin Concerto. Besides, it has a slow movement to die for. The importance of the "Prague" Symphony is mentioned in the previous group. If you like your music big, juicy, complex, and filled to the bursting point with varicolored ideas and expressive nuance, then treat yourself to this set.

Mozart's Top 10 (A Personal Selection)

Divertimento in E flat, K. 563, for string trio
Piano and Wind Quintet in E-flat Major, K. 452
String Quintet in G Minor, K. 516
Clarinet Quintet in A Major, K. 581
Wind Serenade No. 10 in B-flat Major, K. 361 ("Gran Partita")
"Posthorn" Serenade in D Major, K. 320
Symphony No. 38 in D Major, K. 504 ("Prague")
Symphony No. 40 in G Minor, K. 550
Piano Concerto No. 17 in G Major, K. 453
Piano Concerto No. 25 in C Major, K. 503

Here are (very briefly) some of the reasons for my choices:

1. Divertimento in E-Flat for string trio: I am simply aghast with admiration at a work of about three quarters of an hour in length written for only three strings that never once sounds thin in texture or bereft of ideas. The piece is a miracle.

2. Piano and Wind Quintet in E-flat Major: I love the timbre of wind instruments, their vocal character, and the incredibly euphonious sounds that Mozart draws from them here.

3. String Quintet in G Minor: You have to admire the way Mozart writes the saddest music of his career and then says "to hell with it" and gets on with life in the happy finale. That takes both guts and a total absence of self-pity.

4. Clarinet Quintet in A Major: It was in the last episode of *M*A*S*H*. It has to be great.

5. "Gran Partita", a.k.a. Wind Serenade No. 10 in B-flat Major: This is probably the most amiably eccentric piece of music in existence, with a sonority like nothing else on the planet, and it's more fun than music has any right to be.

6. "Posthorn" Serenade in D Major: I couldn't have cared less about this piece until I started working on this book, and now I'm in love.

7. Symphony No. 38 in D Major ("Prague"): I like development sections, and this one has two of Mozart's longest and boldest.

8. Symphony No. 40 in G Minor: Everyone adores it, everyone knows it, cell phones play it. Sometimes the majority does get it right.

9. Piano Concerto No. 17 in G Major: The themes of the outer movements make me laugh. This has sometimes caused problems at concerts.

10. Piano Concerto No. 25 in C Major: This is big, bold, hugely grand, vastly underrated, and magnificently built out of nothing special.

In concluding this survey, I want to stress once again Mozart's concentration on the expression of feelings in his instrumental music as a natural extension of his love of the human voice and of singing. His personal stylistic parameters and the conventions of his day meant that most of the time these were necessarily happy feelings, but they are no less serious for that. Indeed, the romantic myth of the suffering artist-hero expressing personal misery in his creations has always been exaggerated as it relates to music of all periods. What Mozart accomplished above all else was not (as some would maintain) the creation of exceptional musical "depth" through those few minor-key movements and works evocative of sadness and despair. Rather, it was an expressive quality that perhaps can best be summed up by the word "wholeness."

In Mozart's mature work, what distinguishes it from that of almost all of his contemporaries is its range and comprehensiveness, his ability to encompass both happiness and sadness (and every gradation in between) at one and the same time, within the same work, the same movement, or even the same melody. This is a gift. It cannot be learned. Mozart displays this gift through musical content (that is, tunes and motives), through his remarkable command of form, and in particular through those aspects of form that permit him to increase the size of his works, thus providing the space necessary to accommodate the music's large emotional vocabulary.

That said, it's equally important to understand that Mozart does not wear his heart on his sleeve. The emotions he expresses are real enough, but they need not necessarily be *his*. This detachment or objectivity (if you like) permits him to polish his musical surfaces to a fine sheen, to insinuate rather than to shout, to counter pathos with wit, to be wise without preaching, and to mix his musical ingredients like a master chef. Mozart permits himself to go only so far in any one direction, certainly (as he himself famously said) never to the point of offending the ear, no matter how intense the emotion or how densely woven the musical argument. This exquisite sense of balance and proportion is perhaps the most difficult aspect of Mozart's art to grasp, yet it's also one of the most important because his emotional inclusiveness depends on it.

Mozart's musical objectives being largely concerned with capturing in sound the wholeness of the human personality, he almost never indulges in gratuitous technical display for its own sake. It surely would have been easier for him to limit the range of emotions on offer so as to be able express each one more forcefully, as composers of both the baroque and romantic periods liked to do. But to take that road would have meant neglecting too many opportunities to enrich and expand his musical language, to create as much color and contrast as he could, and to leave each work as emotionally complete, psychologically speaking, as possible.

There are other composers, both earlier and later, able to evoke specific feelings with as much or greater intensity, but certainly none before Mozart (and very few after) had as large a repertoire of expressive devices, used them with such a generous hand and with equal success in so many different genres, and in so doing, created music as beguilingly beautiful as it is both smart and emotionally truthful.

Index of Works

Chamber Music

Orchestral Music

Opera Overtures:

Concertos:

CD Track Listing

1. Symphony No. 41 in C Major, K. 551 ("Jupiter"),
    first movement (10:54)

    James Levine, conductor, Chicago Symphony Orchestra

    ℗1982 BMG Music. Courtesy of BMG Classics, a unit of BMG Music.
    From RCA Gold Seal 61397-2.

2. Symphony No. 40 in G Minor, K. 550, first movement (7:14)

    James Levine, conductor, Chicago Symphony Orchestra

    ℗1982 BMG Music. Courtesy of BMG Classics, a unit of BMG Music.
    From RCA Gold Seal 61397-3.

3. Piano Concerto No. 21 in C Major, K. 467
    ("Elvira Madigan"), second movement (7:34)

    Alicia de Larrocha, piano; Sir Colin Davis, conductor, English
    Chamber Orchestra

    ℗1991 BMG Music. Courtesy of BMG Classics, a unit of BMG Music.
    From RCA Red Seal BG2 60825.

4. Piano Concerto No. 17 in G Major, K. 453, finale (7:59)

    Emanuel Ax, piano; Pinchas Zukerman, conductor, Saint Paul
    Chamber Orchestra

    ℗1982 BMG Music. Courtesy of BMG Classics, a unit of BMG Music.
    From RCA Victrola 60136-2-RV.

5. Clarinet Quintet in A Major, K. 581, first movement (9:32)

   Richard Stoltzman, clarinet; Tokyo String Quartet

   ℗1991 BMG Music. Courtesy of BMG Classics, a unit of BMG Music.
   From RCA Red Seal 60723-2-RC.

6. String Quintet in G Minor, K. 516, first movement (11:22)

   Pinchas Zukerman, viola; Tokyo String Quartet

   ℗1992 BMG Music. Courtesy of BMG Classics, a unit of BMG Music.
   From RCA Red Seal 60940-2.

7. Aria: Un Bacio di Mano, K. 541 (2:06)

   Stephan Genz, baritone; Sigiswald Kuijken, conductor,
   La Petite Bande

   ℗2003 BMG Ariola Classics GmbH. Courtesy of BMG Ariola Classics
   GmbH.

   From DHM 55782-2.

8. Violin Concerto No. 5 in A Major, K. 219, finale (6:43)

   Jascha Heifetz, violin, with chamber orchestra

   Originally recorded prior to 1972. All rights reserved by BMG Music.
   Courtesy of BMG Music, a unit of BMG Music.

   From RCA Gold Seal 7869-2-RG.

9. Symphony No. 39 in E-flat Major, K. 543, third movement
   (4:18)

   Günter Wand, conductor, NDR Symphony Orchestra

   ℗1990 BMG Music. Courtesy of BMG Ariola Classics GmbH.
   From RCA Red Seal RD 60714.

10. Serenade No. 10 in B-Flat Major, K. 361 ("Gran Partita"),
    finale (3:33)

    Sir Colin Davis, conductor, Bavarian Radio Symphony Orchestra

    ℗1992 BMG Music. Courtesy of BMG Classics, a unit of BMG Music.
    From RCA Red Seal 60872-2.

11. Don Giovanni, K. 527, Overture (5:48)

Sir Colin Davis, conductor, Staatskapelle Dresden

℗1999 BMG Music. Courtesy of BMG Ariola Classics GmbH.

From RCA Red Seal 56698-2.

11